B4 $11.95

Paul Haesaerts   James Ensor

Paul Haesaerts

James Ensor

Preface by Jean Cassou

Harry N. Abrams, Inc., New York

To Danièle, to Edé

Library of Congress Catalog Card Number: 58–9032
Published in the United States of America, 1959,
by Harry N. Abrams, Inc., New York
All rights reserved. No part of the contents of this book
may be reproduced without the written permission of the publishers
Copyright 1957 in Belgium by Les Éditions et Ateliers d'Art Graphique Elsevier, Paris-Brussels
Milton S. Fox, Editor
Translated from the French by Norbert Guterman
Cover and jacket designed by Theo Kurpershoek
Printed in Germany with the exception of the color plates
which were printed in Belgium

CONTENTS

53115

Preface by Jean Cassou   11

The Capriciousness of Aesthetic Opinion   19
Many Strings to his Bow   23
Ensor and his Critics   26
Childhood and Adolescence   30
The Wonder Shops   36
In the Bosom of the Family   38
At the Brussels Academy   40
Extra-Curricular Activities   42
Ostend, Ensor's Muse   44
The Attic Studio   50
The Somber Period: Middle-Class Interiors   51
The Somber Period: Still Lifes   58
The Somber Period: Portraits   60
The Family Circle   64
From the Dark to the Light, from Realism to Unrealism   68
In Full Creative Swing   74
The Home of the Rousseaus in Brussels   80
Youthful High Spirits   82
Fellow-Painters in Les XX   92
A Hundred-and-One Manners   94
Art as Play   98
Hymns to Light   100
Painter of the Sea   104

Skillful Mixtures   108
Target of Abuse   109
Master Engraver   112

Etchings   113

Drawings, Watercolors, and Charcoals   131

Drawings and Watercolors   133

Painter of Masks   163
The Entry of Christ into Brussels   176
Drunks, Tramps, and Beggars   182
The Weight of the Imponderable   188
Humorous Works   189
A Pointed Pen   194
Anguish and Irony   197
Affinity for Christ   200
Death and the Self   204
The Smell of Death and the Fragrance of the Feast   205
"A Reaction is Beginning to Take Shape . . ."   207
Unexpected Collapse   209
The Last Period   213
Escape into Music   215
Slow Rise to Fame   218
Ensor's Aesthetics   226
A Royal Funeral   230
Ensor and Contemporary Painting   231

Signatures of Ensor   233

Paintings   235

Classified Catalogue   299

Documents   335

Original Writings of Ensor   355

Biographical Summary   362

Bibliography   369

Chronological List of All Works Reproduced   375

Acknowledgments   384

Index of Names   385

The reproductions in this book are referred to by page number; the c. c.-numbers refer to the Classified Catalogue.

PREFACE

The many-sided Paul Haesaerts, writer, aesthetician, art critic, producer of erudite and appealing art films, inspirer of noteworthy artistic enterprises – in short, this great promoter of everything artistic – employs in all his writings a sensual imagistic language which is surely most appropriate for commenting upon the great contribution Flanders has made to world art. Whether the Flemish idiom makes use of epithets or of colors, it reveals the same mechanism of expression: a superabundant vital energy eager to burst into concrete, substantial, and light-giving gestures. Evidence bursts forth, permeated with the testimony it bears, and poses no problem, because all it does is posit itself; and it posits itself totally, without the slightest reticence, and without any undertones of doubt, for it has no undertones. It is fully itself, asserting a self that, according to mood, is splendor-loving, dramatic, lyrical, mysterious, or droll. In other words, this evidence, according to mood, is called Bruegel, Rubens, or Ensor.

So, keep a sharp eye out! It is to the eye that such a potentiality of exteriorization appeals, a potentiality which, in this latest of its realizations, has incarnated itself in our great James Ensor. Yes, "ours," for Haesaerts does me the honor and favor of letting me share his intimacy with this lofty figure whom I have never ceased to cherish and to serve as best I can, from the day I called upon him in his legendary souvenir shop, on a visit that remains one of the dearest memories of my youth. There he was, this bearer of the message of the marvelous – there he will always be – like some old magician surrounded by his fetishes and amulets, drawing fantastic polkas out of his harmonium, echoes of the brassy din of *The Entry of Christ into Brussels*. There he was, and my eyes timidly met his clear sea-blue eyes, and my avid ears perceived no cutting tone, but a charming, bantering laughter. There are paintings we can fully enjoy without ever meeting their author. But Ensor's work is too organically linked with its author for us not to regard ourselves as supremely fortunate in having met him. Painting by this kind of painter, I repeat, is will to evidence, to exteriorization, will to expression. Thus, if we delight in looking at it, we must also feel the need to look at such an artist's will to be seen, in other words, to look upon the man who is possessed of this will. To experience such painting one must go back to its sources, grasp it in all its dynamism, conceive it *in actu*. As will to expression, it falls into the province of what has been called "Expressionism."

Expressionism knew a great vogue during the last half-century all over Europe, but especially in Central Europe. This term, however, is not confined to the brilliant German school; it is also a generic term, and denotes an aesthetic category. There were also French Expressionists, who played their part in the modern French school. Although the Expressionist disposition, the Expressionist mood, does not predominate, there were and there are French Expressionists, and in such profusion that the historical category of Expressionism is inevitably represented in it.

James Ensor holds a prominent place in the historical development of Expressionism in Central Europe, a movement which was brought to birth by the diverse influences of Edvard Munch, Vincent Van Gogh, and Paul Gauguin, and flowered with the Blaue Reiter (the Blue Rider group) and Kandinsky's tumultuous improvisations of the same years. Ensor is one of its masters. But once this classification is granted, I must also refer to all that links him to his own Flanders, to a whole school in which "Expressionism" has constantly, congenitally prevailed as an aesthetic category, in diverse artistic personalities.

Thus, the very nature of Expressionism compels the writer who analyzes it under this aspect to put the emphasis on the personality of the Expressionist artist, on his personal motives, on the sudden, historically abrupt, yet inevitable character of his "genius." This genius is best detached from the historical context, and grasped in its privacy. It is thus that Ensor must continue to be seen, to be seen as I saw him, as the recluse of Ostend, inwardly preoccupied with bringing into the light of day the world he bore within him, with manifesting it. Alas, when I saw him, he had already accomplished this, his world had been created, and my happiness was confined to seeing the man who, dazzling as he still was, had his best work behind him. It is

known, and Haesaerts reminds us of it, that about 1900 Ensor's development suddenly stopped. The causes of this are a matter of conjecture. Perhaps we must assume
that the disposition we call "expressionist" in certain cases manifests itself in sudden,
imperious impulses, and entirely spends itself in them. The ways of genius, particularly of so unmistakable a genius, are unfathomable. And this one manifested itself
beyond all expectations. With Ensor's very first steps as a painter, he anticipated,
and anticipated with astonishing power, the discoveries Vuillard was to make in the
still undiscovered territory of Intimism. At one bound he penetrated its very depths.
An extraordinarily sure instinct led him directly to the marvels and secrets of interiors,
their still shadows, the disquiet, the distress, the demons that hide there. He had the
dowser's gifts, and he did not study to acquire them. They were within him, and they
were put to work in every area of external reality, seizing upon everything unusual
that took place there, bringing it to light, and later, when he felt so inclined, dis-
guising it under the features of sarcastic masks. He liked to play games, to play with
his own fears, for his own amusement, composing stories, dramas, and farces. His
caprice was master over things, for he knew the things – his was an extraordinary
knowledge. But where did he get it from? I know that everything has already been
explained, that everything has been analyzed, and that the critic's business is to explain and analyze the most different works, all the works that artistic creation brings
to him, as candidates before an examining board. But we are compelled in this case
to go back to the old idea of genius, according to which there is in genius something
that cannot be explained or analyzed, so that it is impossible to say of genius that it
is this or that. The genius is inhabited by unknown forces, he bloweth where he
listeth, he goes where he pleases. He has affinities with certain elements of reality, and
it is as though *he* chose *them* in order to reconstruct them, to make of them a unique
world. But he does not really choose them; the communication precedes the choice,
and the whole proceeding is involved in a fatal immanence. The genius is consubstan-
tial with his work.

It is well known that art, like any other operation of the mind, implies premeditation
and calculation. The forms the artist creates can be ordered in genealogies and systems,

and can be catalogued in the terms of historians' history, even in the terms of that supremely historical history which has been called *Geschichte ohne Namen* (history without names). Expressionism, like so many other isms, found its place ready and waiting for it at the appropriate time. But let us drop this point of view, turn our backs on it for a moment, as we turn our backs on museums, libraries, archives, and all the other places where chronicles are stored. Sometimes it is necessary to take other and different things into consideration, something as exceptional as a surprise, as beyond all comparisons and as irreducible to other terms as good luck; whatever it is that men have sought to define in terms of an irresistible, all-powerful will to expression, expression of a unique, gratuitously given world of fantasy – in short, what we have come to call "genius", taking the word in all the naïve breadth of its most romantic, most absolute sense. Ensor's genius and Ensor's world are all of that. This world eludes our neat distinctions, our theoretical controversies, our quarrels over terms, our definitions, including the "definition" we have tried to give it, in our purely intellectual desire to classify. It remains outside all these considerations. Doubtless there are other contemporary works that might be referred to in the same terms, and that are also accounted for by the preposterousness of fates just as intensely personal, by the requirements of similarly whimsical and magical powers. To confine myself to the past, I need only mention Rembrandt, Goya, Edgar Allan Poe.... Above all, I should like to convey that Ensor gives me the same kind of satisfaction, the satisfaction of coming face to face with a man who is like no other man, and who, having chanced to appear out of nowhere in just the one corner of the planet where he did appear, on the North Sea coast, immediately put to work the exceptional faculty that was within him – that of entering into intimate relationship with objects both familiar and incongruous, with pieces of furniture, with city streets, with oysters and cabbages, fish and fishwives, carnival madness, the thick pile of certain rugs, the nacreous shadows cast by shells, the laughter after a drink, the skeleton after a life, and out of all those things, compounded and stirred in a crucible to their quintessence and then distilled to an elixir, creating a *magnum opus* over which the Angel of the Bizarre stands guard forever.

Now let us let the pictures communicate with us, and let us listen to Paul Haesaerts. The cinema, a medium that he handles with meticulousness and ingenuity, has taught him to enter deeply into pictures, to miss nothing that is in them, and to expose their every intention. For Ensor's paintings he has summoned up the words most suitable for their exegesis. He is the best cicerone we could ask for, as we set out on our visit to the immortal master, the old man in his attic studio above the souvenir shop, among his collection of seashells, alone with his ghosts.

Jean Cassou
Chief Curator, Museé National d'Art Moderne, Paris

PORTRAIT OF THE PAINTER IN A FLOWERED HAT (detail, see c. c. 22). 1883

One of several parodies (see pp. 165 and 339) of Rubens' self-portraits. The majestic hat that Rubens usually wore when he painted himself has been replaced by a hat with flowers and feathers, such as was worn with fancy dress at the Mid-Lent Carnival in Belgium. The expression is anxious and sad, sadder than that in the Rubens self-portrait. The absurd hat is a sort of counterpoint, intensifying the vague impression of malaise that suffuses the whole painting. The hat may well have been included because of its pretty colors, but this canvas, which is dated 1883, also marks a change of manner. Ensor's "somber" period is superseded by a "light," ironical period.

The Clock. c. 1880

THE CAPRICIOUSNESS OF AESTHETIC OPINION

From year to year, historical and critical studies define the meaning of Ensor's art with ever greater accuracy, and value it ever more highly. Scorned at the beginning of this century, at mid-century it is carefully studied and honored. Ensor who lived through part of this development himself, could not make it out. He chose to be amused by it.

PORTRAIT OF THE ARTIST AT THE EASEL. 1879

Ensor's first major work – major despite its modest dimensions – a record of keen, searching observation by a nineteen-year-old painter. For the epoch it is a bold manifestation of pictorial freedom. A mediocre, back-dated replica is in the Gallery of Self-Portraits at the Uffizi in Florence (see c. c. 21).

His case is not unique, nor even exceptional. It occurs so often that it would be banal, were it not so surprising each time it happened. At every one of its stages, history modifies the past and proceeds to remold its substance in the light of the latest views. This is truer of our own epoch than of any other, for no other epoch was more shaken by unexpected events, more driven to revolution. Radical as its present revisions may be, they are probably merely the beginning of an even more thorough reappraisal. Thus, under the impact of surging and receding tides of aesthetic opinion, unknown civilizations are disclosed, and others, that seemed secure for all time, are engulfed. Certain aspects of a given period, movement, or individual artist are submerged, others emerge. The expressive distortions of Negro art enjoy increasing favor; the elegant eighteenth-century English portraitists have fallen into disrepute. The *Laocoön*, if it is remembered at all, is ridiculed; the *Calf-Bearer*, rescued from oblivion, is revered. The Nazarene and Pre-Raphaelite schools, formerly adulated, are jeered at; old Catalan painting, and the school of Arcimboldo, once unknown, are passionately admired. Murillo, yesterday celebrated, is today spurned; Georges de La Tour, yesterday scorned, is today exalted. Goya, who not so long ago owed his greatness to his court painting, today owes it to the nightmarish works. The same Nymphéas series, for which Monet was suspected of weakness, causes him today to be acclaimed the prophet of an art that negates "the subject." Ensor, who was first given a dunce cap and then crowned with laurels, was thus subjected to the unpredictable workings of a general law – perhaps a law of chance – whose nature is obscure, but whose moods seem to be most capricious.

MANY STRINGS TO HIS BOW

It is possible that complex, polymorphous minds, provided that their diversity derives from a richness of gifts rather than from an inability to concentrate, are less threatened with oblivion than are one-sided minds. The many-faceted, many-voiced artist, by virtue of the very ambiguities that link him with the basic ambiguity of mankind, has, no doubt, a greater chance to endure and to convey his message to succeeding generations than does the static, single-minded artist. Among the expressions and gestures at his disposal, there are always some that parallel expressions and gestures recently come to be appreciated, newly fashionable, or simply in the air.

Some of our contemporaries, from Stravinsky to Cocteau and Picasso, are of baffling diversity. James Ensor, who came before them, like them roams the mazes of multiplicity, trying to hide, trying to lose himself. (No doubt they all believe, Ensor as well as the others, that individuality is acquired only by shunning the traits of factitious personality, by escaping from it.) Attacked and praised for traits he felt he possessed only partially or momentarily, Ensor turned a deaf ear both to disparagement and to tribute, and his fame, which was late in coming, made him suspicious even after it was firmly established. But he did not despair. He knew that his art held surprises, that what was then considered malice would, in the future, prove to be truth.

And the question arose: Was not this madman superlatively clairvoyant? It turned out that his elusive art easily took the successive hurdles of the passing years. And, each hurdle passed, Ensor came back into view, altered yet familiar, more radiant than ever and yet ready to run away again.

Thus, what happened to Ensor is what happens to most of those who, ill at ease in their epoch, transcend it and continue to live on into later epochs. What he was reproached for, does him credit; what seemed to doom him to oblivion, assures his survival.

PORTRAIT OF THE ARTIST'S FATHER. 1881

Ensor had no knowledge at this time of the best work being done by other painters in Paris and elsewhere, yet he already practiced a kind of constructivism, organizing the picture as a system of geometric planes, which relates his explorations to those of Cézanne. He did not become acquainted with the latter's works until nine years later when Cézanne's "Card Players" was exhibited at Les XX in Brussels.

Gamblers. 1883

ENSOR AND HIS CRITICS

Ensor's shifts of style, which his works record, never ceased to disconcert the public, and even occasionally embarrassed his warmest defenders. Bold, surprising, sometimes irritating, his personal idiom never failed to intrigue and capture the eye. Judgments regarding the value of Ensor's art were formed slowly, gropingly, stimulated by questions colored with skepticism and answers implicit with irony. Cassou sees in him "one of the greatest artists, one of the greatest visionaries of all times." For Alfred H. Barr and William S. Lieberman, Ensor is, with Redon, one of the great masters of imaginative freedom, "at the extreme left of the modern movement." De Ridder gives him a place "among the most magnificent, the most exceptional" – a place which will be universally recognized as his, he thinks, "when history will be written without dogmatic or national bias, and without the narrow-minded and arrogant chauvinism that tends to assign artistic priority to two or three powerful nations." Paul Fierens, too, is full of admiration: after recalling Ensor's many-sidedness, his "richness of form and content," he describes him as one of "the greatest painters ever produced by the modern Western world" and demands that he be treated "as we treat Cézanne, Renoir, or Van Gogh – who are studied without condescension." For René Huyghe, Ensor is a pivotal figure in the history of art: "This artist, often regarded as marginal," he says, "actually played a major part in the vast intellectual and aesthetic movement which, at the end of the nineteenth century, heralded the collapse of the classical and Latin spirit."

Today no work on contemporary art fails to analyze Ensor's contribution to the formation of the modern artistic spirit. Despite his extreme individualism, and no doubt partly because of it, his contribution is an integral part of the evolution of art viewed as a global, universal phenomenon.

A few years ago, what intrigued us were the deeper implications of Ensor's various ventures; today, the underlying meanings of his art as a whole are clear. In the history of art, which has been enriched with so many new conceptions, Ensor's manifold thought occupies an increasingly secure place in the minds of present-day interpreters. However, Ensor seems too independent and too diversified not to move forward from the position he is assigned today. He will probably be assigned others in the future, when inescapable changes shall have taken place in taste and the hierarchy of opinion.

In this book we shall try to view him without preconceived ideas, to watch him in his studio, among his friends, in the various milieus of his own city, country, and epoch, following his work step by step, recording the evolution of his art, taking note of its explicit intentions, and attempting to decipher its secret messages. Such a study will help us to situate the man and the artist, to determine in what way they affect us or remain beyond our grasp, the aspects that still resist classification, and to distinguish between the elements that are perishable and those that are durable, those that are threatened with oblivion and those still capable of resurrection.

VIEW OF THE FLEMISH PLAIN. 1876

Before he attended the Brussels Academy, while still in his teens, Ensor executed a number of small works inspired by the sea, the dunes, and the countryside near Ostend. The treatment of these works is timid and industrious, but they contain in germ the elements that will characterize the major works which are similarly flooded with light and evoke vast spaces.

Boats. c. 1880

CHILDHOOD AND ADOLESCENCE

"I was born at Ostend, on April 13, 1860, on a Friday, the day of Venus. At my birth Venus came toward me, smiling, and we looked long into each other's eyes. She smelled pleasantly of salt water." We shall often quote Ensor's writings. They cast a vivid light on his artistic conceptions, and inform us, more reliably than any other source, of his reactions to the events of his life. The way he speaks of his birth tells us at once how much the charms and, as we will explain later, the odors, the movements, the whims, and the mysteries of the sea, contributed to the fashioning of his artistic ideas.

His earliest childhood memories reflect the changing rhythms of the sea. It was a sea bird, a kind of messenger from the deeps of space and water, that accounts for his strongest early impression – in this case an impression of terror: "One night, as I was lying in my lighted room, with all the windows open onto the sea, a large sea bird, attracted by the light, landed in front of me, knocking against my cradle. I have never been able to forget it; I was beside myself with terror. I can still see the horrible apparition, and feel the shock of that fantastic black bird."

He was sent to school. He hated it. He did not rebel; he stayed there for a time, a stranger, inaccessible, discouraging his teachers by his complete lack of interest. After two years of this routine, he obtained his release. His mother indulged his caprices, "keeping up my strength with frequent doses of pralines and sugar almonds." His father, a "superior" man, ill at ease in life, claimed that it was best to let everyone do what he pleased and what his imagination suggested. James idled away his time, dreaming, roaming the dunes and the old port. He was spared the leveling influence and the emotional restraints of school life. He avidly absorbed everything that happened to come his way: "The mysterious stories about fairies, ogres, and malevolent giants that were told me by an interminably chattering old Flemish servant, kindhearted, wrinkled, with hair all gray and silver, impressed me deeply." On tiny scraps of paper, he began to draw vignettes in pencil and in watercolor. Seeing the boy's delight in painting, his father engaged two local teachers to give him a few lessons. Later James said, recalling them: "They initiated me in a professorial manner into the deceptive stereotypes of their gloomy, narrow-minded, and stillborn trade." However, he acquired a taste for reproducing the scenes about him in timid brush strokes; he did this with so much love that the modest descriptions he thus spelled out escaped banality and became little poems. He knew it: "At the age of fifteen," he writes, "I painted the countryside around Ostend from nature. Those unpretentious little works, painted on pink cardboard with a kerosene solvent, still charm me."

THE LAMP BOY. 1880

The common people occupy an important place in Ensor's work, but less as a social class than as a theme for technical variations, and in the later works, as a means of expressing libertarian opinion. In painting this working-class youth, almost a child, Ensor displayed extreme virtuosity, using his most unctuous impastos, his most subtle grays, his deepest blacks; he makes it a piece of pictorial bravado. The timid souls who could not forever deny the value of Ensor, clung to this canvas as to a life raft. This was the first of his pictures to make its way into a museum, some fifteen years after it had been painted.

THE ROWER. 1883

With its dreamy background and the heaviness of its foreground, "The Rower" is one of Ensor's most suggestive paintings of the sea. More vividly than any other it evokes the rough Ostend of the fishermen, which is in such complete contrast with the colorful Ostend of the vacationers. It clearly heralds, in both its brutality and its refinement, the vision of Permeke, particularly of this painter's Ostend period, when, forty years after Ensor, he executed "Fishermen at the Port" and "Rowers."

Mermaid. Ensor liked to surround himself with such bizarre objects, and was extremely attached to this one. Made in Japan, it consisted of wood, human hair, fish scales, and monkey teeth.

THE WONDER SHOPS

Crammed full of strange objects which, in order to lure buyers, overflowed onto the sidewalk, the four shops kept in turn by James's parents, as well as all those kept by other members of his family, his grandmother, aunts, and uncles, provided Ensor with surroundings which some people might find banal, but which to him were inexhaustibly full of wonders. Is it not a characteristic feature of the artist, who is sometimes insensitive to the most spectacular displays, to be able to make a world out of almost nothing?

In these family shops were stored a heterogeneous mixture of seashells, chinoiseries, porcelains from the East Indies, glass trinkets, beach toys, comical or peasant-made statuettes, stuffed animals, three-masted ship models in bottles, vases, dolls, and "souvenirs of Ostend," objects made to astonish, to intrigue, or to scare, and for the Mid-Lent holiday, masks and tinsel ornaments. The child's imagination was fed by all this rich trumpery. He tells us himself how impressed he was by "a certain dark and frightening attic" – where, probably, damaged and unsold objects were relegated – "full of horrible spiders, curios, shells, plants and animals from exotic climes, fine porcelains, old clothing the color of rust and blood, red and white corals, monkeys, turtles, dried mermaids, and stuffed Chinamen." With his capacity for daydreaming and his lively mind, he probably saw more in them than there was.

Today all critics believe in the stimulating virtue of such objects seen in childhood, and in Ensor's case they wax eloquent. Only Jean Teugels protests: "I say that the shop was but a corridor, that Ensor only passed through it, and that he derives directly from the sea, from the seashells and the sand." Ensor himself both agreed and disagreed. While he always said that the sea was his "great inspirer," he did not deny that he drew some elements of his art from the cheap and glittering bric-à-brac that surrounded him: "In my parents' shop I had seen the wavy lines, the serpentine forms of beautiful seashells, the iridescent lights of mother-of-pearl, the rich tones of delicate chinoiseries . . . ." The modest shop – which, incidentally, may itself appear as an emanation, a creation of the sea – thus seems after all to have been a kind of *cabinet de curiosités*, or, as the Germans would say, a *Wunderkammer*, where the explorer's mind found nourishment and exaltation. A poor, shoddy thing, if you like, but to a dreamer and inventor, a springboard.

James was the family's favorite. He was free to do as he liked. He knew no constraint, he was loved by all around him. His sister, a girl who tended to have her head in the clouds, was a diverting companion. His mother, his aunts, and especially Aunt Mimi who lived with them, spoiled him thoroughly. His father secretly thought highly of his gifts, and saw to it that he was left completely free.

The days passed monotonously in the peaceful resort town. Summer brought a spell of surface animation, but in winter the town fell back into its accustomed lethargy. Family life was spent in relative isolation. It could be stifling. The child was aware only of its charms.

To be sure, when he grew older, James noticed that the household had its stormy moments, but during his adolescent years he was entirely absorbed in his own enthusiasms and fears. He was full of ardor, and his wonderment before the spectacle of life did not flag. He lived absent-mindedly, wholly caught up in his own projects, in which he assigned imaginary roles to all those about him, who surrounded him with such warm affection.

Toward 1930 he wrote of his father: "My paternal grandparents had money and spent part of the year on the continent. My father, their eldest son, was born in Brussels, and he was the only one of the six children to live in Belgium. He was brought up there as well as in England. He began medical studies at Bonn and Heidelberg, and then returned to England, where he was employed by an engineer. It was while he was accompanying his parents on a vacation at Ostend that he met his future wife. My father had intellectual interests. He was very sensitive, very gentle, a little haughty with some people. His moral principles were of the highest. He possessed great muscular strength. He was made for a life of action, or at least for sports. He was an excellent swimmer. I remember that on one occasion, while we were walking together, he jumped fully dressed into the sea and swam the full distance between two jetties. At the same time, he was fond of music, and he could draw. He seemed out of his element in the Ostend of that day, a small walled town. In the end he left for the United States in the hope of finding a position there. The Civil War broke out a few months later and changed his plans. He came back to Ostend discouraged, and resigned himself to spending the rest of his life there."

Later, James Ensor was to speak nostalgically of those blessed years of happy family life, the years before awareness came, and before bitterness.

Music, Rue de Flandre. 1890

The Pilgrims at Emmaus (after Rembrandt). c. 1880

AT THE BRUSSELS ACADEMY

"The moment I enrolled, a great misunderstanding occurred. I was told to paint the bust of Octavian, the most illustrious of the Caesars, from a brand-new plaster cast. The snow-white plaster dismayed me." His father had given James permission to attend courses at the Brussels Academy. The atmosphere of the school had a chilling effect on him. "Terrorized, I drove myself too hard. I painted mornings, attended classes in composition in the afternoon, drew in the evening, and at night I mapped out dreams for the future. My teachers, preoccupied, and frowning with disapproval, disparaged me as 'an ignorant dreamer.'" He was up against three "dissimilar teachers": Joseph Stallaert was a belated romantic; Jef Van Severdonck, a painter of heroic military feats; and Alexandre Robert, an emphatic celebrator of the nation's glories. Ensor had his revenge on them when he ridiculed them in an essay published in 1884, which was not well received. On the other hand, the director of the Academy, Jean Portaels, who played in Belgium a role similar to that played later by Gustave Moreau in Paris, found favor in his eyes: "Jean Portaels, who taught our best modern painters, was an exceptional artist. He was expert in rendering the scent of femininity and the charms of soft flesh. *Theater Party in Budapest*, the outstanding work of this painter of the passionate and elegant daughters of Lot and Zion, still holds its interest after all these years."

James won the second prize in drawing for his studies from the classical bust, the only distinction awarded him during his stay at the Academy. One of his sketches, the *Mystic Death of a Theologian* (fancifully entitled *Exalted Monks Reclaiming the Body of the Theologian Sus-Oris Despite the Opposition of the Bishop F (T)riton or F(T)riston*) intrigued Portaels, who kept it in his studio, wondering whether a new spirit was not beginning to be felt in painting.

Ensor was one of those who arrive at knowledge without formal study. The constraints imposed by his teachers weighed heavily on him. Soon he rejected them entirely: "In 1880, I walked out on that establishment for the near-blind, without further ado." And he adds: "I have never been able to understand why my teachers were so upset by my restless explorations. I was guided by a secret instinct, a feeling for the atmosphere of the sea coast, which I had imbibed with the breeze, inhaled with the pearly mists, soaked up in the waves, heard in the wind." He went back to Ostend where a studio awaited him in the family home, and where, alone and free, he was now to devote himself to painting with happy frenzy.

In the meantime he had made many friends in Brussels. Thanks to his classmates, "Khnopff, Evrard, Crespin, and a few other naughty boys champing at the bit," thanks above all to Théo Hannon, dilettante painter and writer, he had joined a stormy, daring, irreverent circle with which he now kept in touch. Some of these men would come to visit him in Ostend, and he regularly visited Brussels, where the small group of friends was preparing to found Les XX and the magazines *La Jeune Belgique* and *L'Art Moderne*.

EXTRA-CURRICULAR ACTIVITIES

In Brussels Ensor avidly sought intellectual nourishment. He "devoured" Poe, Balzac, Heine, Baudelaire, Cervantes, Rabelais, and many other authors whose visions of the world were more or less akin to his own. Later, absorbed entirely in his own creations, he was to read less. But he always stood out among the painters of his time, who were generally distrustful of all intellectuality, by the extent and originality of his culture.

He was just as eager to become acquainted with the work of his predecessors. Recently a number of rapidly drawn, expressive, and skillful copies by Ensor, dating from his years at the Academy, have come to light. His models were of a high technical excellence; Hals, Rembrandt, Goya, Watteau, Daumier, Delacroix, Millet, Manet, Constable, Turner, Callot, as well as unknown artists, provided the occasions for brilliant exercises which Ensor executed with great freedom, aiming only at intensity. Even these early works bear the imprint of Ensor more markedly than they bear that of the artists who inspired him. In these drawings he inaugurated the style of "creating on the basis of the already created," or working "in the manner of . . ." which many artists were subsequently to adopt as a mode of expression.

But the three most important works, already major works, that Ensor executed while he was still a student, are his three self-portraits of 1879 (p. 21, c. c. 19, 20). Very small in size, they are works surprising by both an aesthetic and psychological richness. These first glances that Ensor cast at the world and at himself tell us a great deal about the wonderment, the anxiety if not the fear, with which he vibrantly approached life, as well as about his gift for communicating his emotions by organizing forms and variations of light.

LADY WITH A FAN. 1880

Ensor was twenty when he painted this figure, a portrait of his sister in an evening gown. In contrast to the many portraits of society women in which Alfred Stevens specialized at the time, the portrait done by young Ensor, which gives us a preliminary taste of his future portraits, rises above descriptive and anecdotal realism. He re-creates the subject by building it up in terms of masses and tones which echo one another.

In Ostend, a city where the weather is fickle, Ensor found his true physical climate, a natural environment with the food to nourish his roots, and to stimulate the flowers of his imagination. From his childhood, his lungs, his nerves, and his brain had been steeped in the air of Ostend, iodized, marine, sparkling, swept by the wind. The pattern of life in Ostend was a mixture of conventionality and rudeness, of folklore and petty bourgeois traditions, influenced by aristocrats and foreigners alike, by men in tail coats, fishermen's blouses, and bathing suits. It acquainted him with human passions. The spirit of art is embodied in flesh, and the flesh of Ensor's art is that of his city. It is not surprising that his affection for it never ran dry. He addressed hymns to it: "Ostend, sovereign fairy of skies and multicolored waters. – Ostend, bouquet of joy, of freshness, of health, and vigorous humanity. – Ostend, strange city. Painters' paradise. Blonde goddess of light. Ostend, I have drunk of your pure and salty milk, the milk of the sea . . . ." Throughout his life, in every period of his work, in his letters, his conversations, and his articles, his love for Ostend asserts itself, bursting out again and again.

Ostend had many attractions for its painter – the countryside surrounding it, crowned and exalted by enormous clouds and vast luminous expanses; its softly undulant dunes capped with sea grasses; its shifting skies; the enlarging presence of the sea; its winter fogs and bluster; the band concerts during the summer months; the teeming colors and smells of its crowded docks; the blunt speech of its people; the raciness of its indigenous life seasoned with cosmopolitanism; the comic strangeness of the watering season; its annual Carnival with joyous masks against a background of sadness; the frenzy of storms alternating with moments of total and silken calm. Each of these aspects of Ostend is matched by an aspect of Ensor's art.

One proof of Ensor's attachment to his native city is provided by the energy with which he opposed rebuilding and modernization: "Poor old Ostend, at the mercy of the depredations of lame architects who see no farther than their noses. Down with those who are ruining our marvelous landmarks! Unmask the moldy schemes of the improvement-mad! Blast those who are filling in our wonderful ship basins! Public flogging for those who are leveling the gentle curves of our sand dunes!"

RUE DE FLANDRE IN THE SNOW. 1880

RUE DE FLANDRE IN THE SUN. 1881

Very thinly painted, this canvas suggests rather than depicts. Ensor was never more joyfully impressionistic. In all his other pictures, secondary intentions are explicit or implicit, preventing him from being a full-fledged Impressionist. The changes of season are accompanied in Ensor by basic changes in style and technique. He paints winter scenes and snow in the manner of Vogels, applying the paint in succulent thick layers with a palette knife. This work should be compared with a painting of the same street in the snow (see p. 45) and in summer, filled with musicians (see p. 49). Other Ostend streets are treated, according to the time of day, in manners recalling Symbolism, heralding Fauvism, or returning to Constructivism.

MUSIC, RUE DE FLANDRE. 1891

There is not a trace of impressionistic imprecision in this picture. The rhythm of the forms suggests the staccato precision of a military march. By his manner of painting Ensor suggests here the bursts of music bouncing from the housefronts. This picture heralds the intensity, the joy, and the freshness of the Fauves (see pp. 45 and 47). It is a member of a brilliant line of paintings: the cobblestone street was treated as subject by Manet and Monet in 1878, by Van Gogh in 1886, by Dufy and Marquet in 1906, and by Léger in 1914.

THE ATTIC STUDIO

In order to paint without interruptions, when he came back to Ostend, James moved into a sort of attic or loft at the top of a corner building several stories high, which his parents had leased. On the ground floor, as usual, they set up their souvenir shop, and during the season they rented out most of the other rooms in the building to vacationists. From his attic studio – which, aside from a few "bull's-eyes" or portholes, was lit only by one quite small square window in the sloping wall of the gabled façade – James could see the sky and the rooftops of Ostend. He could also look down into the Rue de Flandre and the Boulevard Van Iseghem. By leaning out of the window he could catch a glimpse of the sea, only a hundred yards or so from the house. The sound of the surf, whether a gentle strumming or a roar of pounding breakers, was always present in the studio. Occasionally, in quest of a particular background or a particular model, he would move his easel into one of the rooms occupied by his parents, his aunt, or his sister. At other times, a canvas under his arm, he would go out to paint the sea, the dunes, or the countryside. But the attic was where he worked most often, where he planned, meditated, and stored his work. There, he was capable of working for long periods in a veritable frenzy. Outwardly, his days passed peacefully and almost monotonously, and yet, what was going on in that attic studio during the twenty years from 1880 to 1900 – the only years of Ensor's long career that really matter – was extraordinarily significant in the history of modern painting. In that retreat a man was giving himself unreservedly, and with perfect self-mastery, to the spirit of adventure, to the joy of creation. To some extent the future of modern painting was determined in that attic.

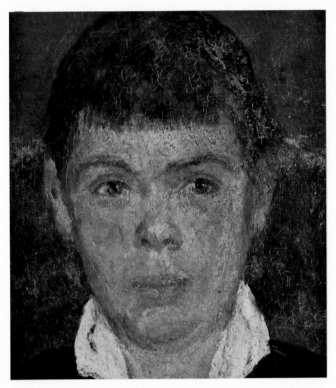

GIRL WITH THE TURNED-UP NOSE (detail, see c. c. 1). 1879

The people whom Ensor portrayed at the beginning of his career, like the figures in his realistic interiors, were those he observed at leisure in his immediate surroundings at Ostend. The "Girl with the Turned-Up Nose" was a servant in Ensor's parents' house. Her face gave James an opportunity to study the subtle variations of color in filtered light of low intensity.

THE SOMBER PERIOD: MIDDLE-CLASS INTERIORS

Ensor's creative method was that of transcendence and sublimation. He appeared on the historical scene "at the moment when the ripe cheese of realism smelled good," in a period of "rich impastos, gorgeous scrawls, luscious patinas, crusty ragouts. The

51

tubes of silver white spat forth cream, and the whole – impasto, crust, and colors – was carefully and completely covered with genuine varnish." Far from disavowing this kind of painting, Ensor practiced it with consummate skill, with more gusto than anyone else. His *Lamp Boy* (p. 33), his portrait of the painter Willy Finch (p. 63, c. c. 7), and a good number of other canvases are made up of succulent, flowing colors, of forms drowned in thick layers of rich warm oil paint. But virtuosity of itself and for itself left him dissatisfied, and "realism," as it had been understood before him and was practiced around him, seemed to him an obstacle to perceiving "true reality." He located the latter somewhere beyond the barrier wall of "realism," which he conceived as a limit that had to be broken through. Throughout this period of his development, which, despite everything, may as well be called "realist," Ensor often found his way through that wall that had proved impassable for so many others. Later, he was to explore only the territory beyond this confining wall, and everything on this side of it would come to seem alien to him.

The objects and personages in his "middle-class interiors," in *Russian Music* (p. 249), *Afternoon at Ostend* (pp. 53, 55), *Bourgeois Salon* (p. 248), *Somber Lady* (p. 57), *The Colorist* (p. 254), *Lady in Distress* (p. 264), are not instantly or immediately apprehended. While representing them in all their material reality, Ensor situates them, by the magic of his art, outside time and space. A light that seems to come from the sea, or from sidereal space, seeps through the tulle curtains, caresses the hangings, glides over the porcelains, spills over onto the furniture and rugs, and penetrates the very souls of those who are in the rooms. Everyday life is somehow transformed into a world all its own, a world of silence and mystery. Seeds of doubt had been sown as to the reality of the "real." Ensor waited for those seeds of uncertainty which he planted to sprout and grow, and later he went on to paint invisible presences, phantoms about to step out from the curtains and to writhe on the floor, teasing and intriguing the mortal beings already there. This perception of a *tangible* mystery that was to be so strongly realized in *Haunted Furniture* (c. c. 127) makes itself felt in the earlier *Afternoon at Ostend* and other paintings of middle-class interiors. Some insidious disquiet is visited upon them, a sort of mist settles down, reminiscent of the "spleen" of a

Baudelaire, a Mallarmé, or a Laforgue. We seem to be listening to Maeterlinck's line, "Have pity on all airless, closed spaces."

Technically, this swallowing-up of conventional reality is rendered by means of Ensor's close study of form and by his parallel study of the disintegrating action of light, jumbling and distorting the forms. In his attempts to express mystery, Ensor, unlike Van Gogh in his early works and unlike Permeke later, never resorts to all-but-total darkness. Actually we should not speak of a "somber" or "dark" period in his case, save in so far as these early works contrast with the extreme intensity of certain canvases of the later, so-called "light" period.

AFTERNOON AT OSTEND (see detail p. 55). 1881

AFTERNOON AT OSTEND (detail, see p. 53)

Posed by the artist's sister and mother, this rigorously composed painting is no doubt the most important of the "somber" period. A version that dates from about 1910 transposes it entirely into a range of brilliant light tones (see p. 222).

SOMBER LADY. 1881

Here, too, Ensor used his sister as his model. This work belongs to the series of middle-class interiors.

THE SOMBER PERIOD: STILL LIFES

The strangeness of objects, however ordinary or extraordinary they might be, never failed to intrigue and stimulate Ensor's mind. In countless sketches, most often executed in colored crayon, he tried to render the texture and substance, the very expressions worn by penknives, by the knobs and whorls of furniture, by lamps, bunches of keys, inkstands, faucets, crumpled paper, by lanterns, ship models, fans, old shoes, watches, vases – by an inanimate world that he infuses with life and charges with passion, transposing it into a realm of the unusual.

At the same time he painted, in glittering impasto often laid on with the palette knife, a series of still life compositions which reveal him as a virtuoso in the art of rendering materials: the transparency of glass, the glow of brass, the stiffness of vegetable stems, the rough textures of baskets and straw, the coldness of a plucked fowl, the smoothness of cloth, the high polish of porcelain and the insides of sea shells. The chemistry and physics of the objects are constitutive elements in the picture. This is the period when Ensor, along with Cézanne but in a different spirit, set out in quest of form by way of color. But the parallel preoccupations of the two painters soon diverge. Whereas Cézanne was increasingly to emphasize the palpable, physically most stable elements, Ensor more and more concerned himself with the impalpable, the fluid, with the underlying realities. Charles Sterling notes this tendency in Ensor's still life compositions: "From then on, in both the thickly and thinly applied areas of paint, we detect a fantastic spirit that seeks to expose certain disquieting appearances in nature. Among the fishes, Ensor favors the skate, with its little human mask: in 1882 he painted one lying on a bed of straw that forms, as it were, a tissue of asbestos flakes, a formless accumulation of white fluorescence out of which two piercing eyes gleam; then years later he painted another, more realistic in the flaccidity of its flesh, but more grotesque in its brightly colored iridescence, and above all, more monstrously human, with its cruel and ironical face" (pp. 261, 278).

And he goes on to say: "Like all great still-life painters, Ensor both created his own repertory of objects and gave them new meaning." This is true even of the so-called somber period, when he painted *The Blue Flagon* (see below) with its withered chicken carcass; it is truer still of the period later on when he painted *Attributes of the Studio* (p. 97), which shows a more than naked anatomical dummy, a wretched human marionette surrounded by grimacing apparitions; *Flowers and Vegetables* (p. 73, c. c. 113), with its radiant sunflower, an image of light; and *Seashells* (p. 71), those seashells whose pink mouths whisper the sounds of the sea, and whose furrowed backs mimic the troughs of the waves.

THE BLUE FLAGON. 1880

This subtle and vigorous piece is a fine specimen of the series of still-life compositions in subdued tones that Ensor painted in 1880 and 1881. In each of them the painter practices his scales, so to speak, in order to perfect his skill at imprinting his conceptions on objects. There are several versions of this painting; the one shown here is the first, and the most accomplished.

THE SOMBER PERIOD: PORTRAITS

It was during his "somber" period that Ensor painted his most remarkable portraits, his only portraits, one might say, for later he painted fewer, and they have a predominantly satirical, anecdotal character. The earlier ones are portraits in the true sense of the word; their attraction and significance derive from the presence of a human being whose psychology is defined and translated into terms of pictorial poetry. Like almost all great occasional portraitists, Ensor took as his models persons he knew well: his sister, his mother, his father, himself (there are many self-portraits), the hired girl who inspired *Girl with the Turned-Up Nose* (p. 51, c. c. 1), Charlotte and other young women who worked in the family shop, and finally his painter friends, Willy Finch, Théo Hannon, Guillaume Vogels, Dario de Regoyos. And should we not include among the portraits, the figures represented in the middle-class interiors, all of whom were relatives or close friends? His purpose in these works is to carry further an analysis of given individuals, and, ultimately, to complete the portrait by placing his sitter within his habitual surroundings, as an organic extension of his mentality. This was what Degas did, and what Vuillard was to do later. In this conception, the portrait is simultaneously the image of a person and of a society, of a social class.

The first portraits, those he painted of himself as a student, are accomplished works that inaugurate the series and determine its character. They reveal the artist in a state of clairvoyance: his other models, however wrapped in mystery they may be, are less aware. The disquiet that surrounds and penetrates them is not their own, but something that dwells in the painter, of which they are unconscious, but which nevertheless concerns them. The poses are by no means unusual. The models are usually seated and shown full face. There are no special props, and the faces show no particular expression. But each person portrayed is impressive merely by his presence, and it is his moral weight that invests the picture with its characteristic atmosphere and intensity. The names of Rembrandt, Goya, and Manet have been mentioned in connection with these works. Yet in these portraits Ensor shows himself to be more capable of surprise and less in love with his subjects than Rembrandt. He is less malicious than Goya, more complex and less relaxed than Manet. While there are features in which he resembles these great painters – *Portrait of the Artist's Mother* (p. 245), for example, is almost a Goya, *Portrait of the Painter in a Flowered Hat* (p. 17, c. c. 22), almost a Rembrandt, and *The Lamp Boy* (p. 33) almost a Manet – still in all of them, even in the earliest of these works, he also displays personal characteristics which will set him off from the others still more in the later periods, when his originality will have developed fully.

The portraits mark Ensor's first contact with the human being. He invested them with a dignity rooted in his admiration for life, and with the capacity for transfiguration inherent in his art. Now, he would go on to judge that human being.

THE PAINTER WILLY FINCH (detail, see c. c. 7). 1882

A close friend of Ensor's, the painter Finch battled alongside the other members of Les XX against what he called "officialism"; in 1888 he joined the Pointillists, and left Belgium for his native Finland, where he became a ceramist, and painted landscapes that were increasingly austere. Ensor used him frequently as a model, made several portraits of him, and represented him in his painting "Russian Music" (p. 249). This portrait is one of those in which Ensor is at his best in showing the play of light and shadow on the human face, their assonances or dissonances, their oppositions and reconciliations.

Sloth. c. 1890

THE FAMILY CIRCLE

Some of Ensor's writer friends have left us brief portraits of him, as he was at the beginning of his career. "He was tall and slender," says Grégoire Le Roy, "but pale and excessively thin, so pale and so thin that his fellow townsmen nicknamed him the Grim Reaper (in Ostend dialect, *Pietje-de-dood*)." Camille Mauclair writes: "He has the gentleman's discreet and courteous irony, and a kind of elegant reserve that I have encountered in no one else, combining Spanish pride, English phlegm, and the detachment of the habitual dreamer." Lemonnier speaks of him as a "big, melancholy Pierrot, passing through life as though hallucinated."

Both shy and irreverent, he had bursts of aggressiveness. His prolonged silences could be disquieting; his outbursts, which sometimes took the form of unexpectedly embarrassing remarks, sometimes of furious poundings on the piano, were disconcerting. A study of his self-portraits, of the deep-set eyes and the receding chin that was shortly to be concealed by a beard, suggests a lack of will power. He was sensitive, easily frightened, and easily hurt. His mind was constantly on the alert, his imagination wayward and irreverent. His eyes were fixed on distant horizons, and he saw what no one else could see. In his thoughts he soared far above the plane of the immediate.

Around him, unfortunately, in most of his fellow painters, in his city, and within his own family circle, pettiness prevailed. Besides lack of understanding there was worse, mediocrity. He suffered from it and tried to resist it. His horror of the banal was such that he was all but unaware of the platitudinous; yet his unsparing lucidity made it impossible for him not to be aware of it. Domestic storms were constantly breaking out within the family circle. His mother had a ready store of recrimination: she distrusted everything and everyone, and did her best to set son against husband. The latter, an essentially frustrated and unhappy man, rebelled in vain, lashing about like a wild beast in a cage. James's sister got away from the house at every opportunity. His aunt was given to highly vocal self-pity. Even the moments of relative calm were heavy with the boredom peculiar to provincial life.

James gave himself up entirely to the exaltation of work. As Schneider says of Jules Renard, for "real hells" he substituted "artificial paradises." All the more painful, then, were the returns to humdrum everyday existence. The fact that Ensor found no moral support anywhere in his own country, in his city, or in those around him, moved Verhaeren to say: "Like the grain of some rare and precious wood, his delicate sensitivity was bruised and scraped by contact with stupidity. He felt stepped on, pushed around, broken." Ensor must have felt something of what Rimbaud felt – Ostend was surely no better than Charleville – when he exclaimed: "I am dying, rotting away in all this platitude, shoddiness, and colorlessness . . . . The spirit of the population is an abominable prurigo of idiocy . . . . It's amazing, the things one hears. It undermines you." Henceforward Ensor will see the world under a different aspect, and take up a new attitude toward it, an attitude mingling sarcasm, indifference, revenge, and sadness. Now, all his art takes on that tone. There will be more and more canvases representing grotesque combats, mad, whimsical, ridiculous scenes that should perhaps be regarded as reflecting the banal disputes and petty quarrels which, helpless and disgusted, he had been forced to listen to.

OSTEND ROOFTOPS. 1898

The roofs of Ostend, which Ensor painted many times from his attic studio, are for the most part submerged in the mist of an iridescent light, a feature recalling Turner and the last works of Monet. However, attentive as he is to atmospheric variations, Ensor occasionally forgets the fluid and disintegrating light, rendering it, as he does here, crystalline in its brilliance, and outlining the forms with great sharpness.

FROM THE DARK TO THE LIGHT,
FROM REALISM TO UNREALISM

All in all, Ensor's somber period did not last more than four years, from 1879 to 1882. In 1883 there appeared the first well-pronounced symptoms of a new orientation. The famous *Portrait of the Painter in a Flowered Hat* (p. 17, c. c. 22), dating from that year, may, in this respect, be considered a pivotal canvas, an important transitional work. Atop a face submerged in shadow, eyes sorrowful and questioning – his own face – the artist set a fantastic hat with absurd ornaments, flowered and feathered, a hat in faded Carnival colors. The mist-shrouded period is now crowned by a light period, gaily fantastic and pervaded with an ambiguous joyfulness. In the interval between the two, the uncertain lighting of the middle-class interiors had shaken off mists and dust, and acquired pearly and vivid tones, in the sky above the *Ostend Rooftops* (pp. 67, 253), down by the docks where the *Seashells* (p. 71) lie piled, and in the heavens where the *Fall of the Rebellious Angels* (p. 79) takes place. The light canvases grew organically out of the somber ones; gleaming new shoots and flowers of pure color, sprang from their earthy roots. Like Turner, like Manet, Van Gogh, and Matisse, like so many other painters eager to capture light, Ensor began in the element of darkness and slowly felt his way through the twilight tones; and as soon as he had surmounted an initial shyness, he gradually developed a fondness for the diaphanous, for the most brilliant lighting. Nothing reveals this development better than the successive treatments by various techniques of the same subject. The same Rue de Flandre, first painted by Ensor in winter (p. 45), a street deserted and dark despite the snow that has fallen, is in later versions flooded with a delicate spring sun (p. 47), and we see it finally crowded with musicians in close ranks, brasses sounding lustily, in the key of the implacable summer daylight (p. 49).

But let there be no misunderstanding: there is no clean-cut break. What we witness time and again, rather, is a blending of the two orientations. Something of Fantin-

Latour's subtle grisaille blends with something of Dufy's scintillation. Something of Renoir's joyousness is mingled with something of Rembrandt's sadness. Laughter and anguish rub elbows. For, in addition to a new technical orientation we have here a new way of looking at life, one that is, of course, inseparable from its pictorial expression. The trinkets of the flowered hat, precursors of the more radiant colors to come, are also heralds of irony, of greater freedom, of bolder inventions, of grotesque scenes, of a growing predilection for the playful, the gratuitous, the absurd. Realism, which had already been seriously discredited, would one day be replaced by unrealism, that is to say, by a refusal to accept life in terms of external appearance. This was to lead Ensor to a baffling diversity; his art will explode in every sense, like a fireworks display with endless surprises.

Old Woman Asleep. c. 1893

STILL LIFE WITH FRUIT. 1889

The subtleties of the colors, their hesitations, their shifts, describe the transparency of the glass and the light, evoke the fragrance of tired leaves, the savor of the juices, and the flesh of the fruits. This canvas has sometimes been referred to as "Still Life with Parrot;" the outline of a parrot which has been eliminated from the picture can be made out at the right where it was painted over.

SEASHELLS. 1895

Against a background of marine space, there is a bouquet, a pyramid of shells and crustaceans, some enormous and some quite tiny, that seem to owe their existence, their fantastic forms, their nacreous tones, their textures to the sand, wind, waves, and light. Here Ensor no longer paints the form – the form bursts into flower before our eyes.

71

FLOWERS AND VEGETABLES (detail, see c. c. 113). 1896

Ensor occasionally introduced Japanese fans, trinkets, and screens into the still-life compositions of his "somber" period. In this one there are no Oriental objects, but in the lightness of the technique, in the twisted forms, and in a certain mannerism it reminds of the Japanese. Thus Ensor reveals an interest shared by other painters of the period, by Van Gogh in his "Flowering Pear Tree" and "Père Tanguy," and by Toulouse-Lautrec and Bonnard in their posters.

IN FULL CREATIVE SWING

If Ensor had produced only his "somber" canvases, we would see in him a great painter who, adopting a manner already in vogue, made better use of it than anyone else had done – even renewing its spirit. But he would not then appear to us so extraordinary an inventor.

When he painted *Intrigue* (pp. 85, 86, 87), *Old Woman with Masks* (p. 89, c. c. 130), *The Despair of Pierrot* (p. 91), *The Entry of Christ into Brussels* (pp. 181, 274, 275), and so many other highly original works, he contributed absolutely new elements to art, elements pertaining to sensory perception, subject matter, and the utilization of pictorial language.

It is possible that, challenged by the lack of understanding that surrounded him and disgusted by his family, he took refuge in the fantastic, and clung to the imaginary as to a life preserver. However, in his attic so close to the sky and so near the sea he was able to keep on working, and after a period of experimentation (which itself accounts for some valuable canvases) he produced a magnificent series of disconcerting masterpieces.

His new bent seems to have filled him with explosive energy. He had been naively in love with the world around him, even enthusiastic about it, seeking nothing from it save artistic inspiration. Now he was still in love with the world, but he brought to bear on it an extremely keen vision, which exposes its misery, its ridiculousness, its absurdity. And in his mind he laughed – or pretended to laugh – at both his own anguish and at human restlessness and foolishness in general, at the fate – at once dramatic and grotesque – of mortal man. In the course of the following years, he was to express this new vision with all the fire of his youth, with all the power and subtlety of an exceptionally gifted painter.

Self-Portrait. 1885

THE TRIBULATIONS OF SAINT ANTHONY. 1887

While the subject of this painting derives from a tradition that goes back, through Flaubert, to Callot, Teniers, and Bosch, the treatment and conception in terms of the pictorial medium, in oil and color, are exclusively Ensor's. "His brush swirls and slashes over his canvas with a freedom which matches the audacity of his imagination," observes Alfred H. Barr, Director of the Collections of the Museum of Modern Art in New York. And he adds: "Indeed, at this moment in his career, Ensor was possibly the boldest living painter."

CHRIST IN AGONY. 1888

Many of Ensor's tiniest works, thanks to their pictorial magic, suggest a physical and a spiritual breadth that infinitely transcends their modest dimensions. There are several replicas of this work, which are back-dated and of inferior quality.

FALL OF THE REBELLIOUS ANGELS. 1889

The subject is almost entirely disregarded – more accurately, it is expressed solely in the eloquent colors and brush-strokes. Here Ensor is precursor to such non-figurative lyrical painters as Bazaine, Hartung, and Pollock.

THE HOME OF THE ROUSSEAUS IN BRUSSELS

Ensor's new spiritual orientation was a reaction against the stifling atmosphere surrounding him in Ostend; but in Brussels, in a milieu characterized by warm cordiality and the greatest intellectual freedom, he was warmly received and stimulated further. This was the circle around Ernest Rousseau, professor of physics, specialist in weights and measures, Rector of the University of Brussels. Ensor was introduced there by Théo Hannon, high-spirited comrade, painter and writer, a brother of Madame Rousseau's. They met at Camille Van Camp's studio where they both worked for a year. Ernest Rousseau, a corpulent man with a thick, drooping mustache (Ensor has immortalized him in a magnificent etching, p. 114) was liked by everyone he met. Tolerant, a scoffer at the authorities, infectiously kindhearted, he combined a universal culture with solid peasant simplicity. (He was originally from the village of Marche.) His cheerful and enterprising wife Mariette, nineteen years younger than he, daughter of an eminent botanist, was interested in science and ideas; she spent hours on end peering through the miscroscope. Ensor made a drawing of her in that pose. She was also an art lover, and Ensor's paintings enchanted her.

Although the Rousseaus were not in any way worldly, they played host to a large number of friends. Their house, at No. 20 Rue Vautier, adjoined the Museum of Natural History and the Antoine Wiertz museum. The strangeness of these museums, one of which contained all sorts of oddities of nature – gigantic prehistoric monsters and minuscule monsters of the insect world – and the other, oddities collected by the eccentric Wiertz, amused and intrigued Ensor. The Rousseaus were on the whole inclined to anarchism and atheism, but the persons who frequented their home held the most divergent opinions. Among them were Félicien Rops, satirical and satanical draftsman, much in vogue in Paris; his son-in-law Eugène Demolder, a merry fellow, lazy and gluttonous, refined man-of-letters, one of Ensor's favorite companions; General Leman, who had an amusing running quarrel with Ensor; the brothers Reclus, who were enthusiastic geographers as well as notorious anarchists, and whose sister Louise Dumesnil was Mariette Rousseau's close friend. The Rousseaus had a son, also named Ernest, who studied medicine; though twelve years younger than Ensor, he became the artist's closest friend. A niece, Blanche Rousseau, brought up a Catholic, was treated like a member of the family. Her father, J. B. Rousseau, *directeur général* at the Ministry of Fine Arts, disliked Ensor's painting, but Blanche, who developed into a writer of delicate sensibility, greatly admired this friend of the Rousseau family. She speaks warmly of their first meeting: "I can still see that tall figure, pale in his black clothes, standing alone in a dark corner, and hesitantly extending an elegant hand – and above all, his quick, inquiring glance from those extraordinary eyes, at once shy, provocative, gentle, sarcastic, and shifty, rapidly raised and lowered, while his huge, rigid body made an awkward bow. He had the face of a mocking Christ or a nostalgic Satan. He spoke of the devil in a low voice. I was still a child; this evocation of the devil filled me with vague fear. Insensibly bending toward him, I heard him say that the devil had been following him through the streets, and that he was a suspicious-looking little fellow who kept peeking at you with one eye."

Ensor was a frequent guest in this cheerfully hospitable, and stimulating house. Coming from Ostend where he had been secluded in his studio, he would stay on for weeks and sometimes for months. There was a room always at his disposal, where he could work.

Mariette Rousseau was his "good fairy." She understood him, encouraged him, and urged him to keep working, for he was often hesitant, full of fears, easily discouraged. She bought some of his pictures; one of them, *The Colorist* (p. 254), she bought the moment it was finished. She scolded him when, short of money, he painted over his old canvases. She was confidante, protector, one who could both allay his fears and keep up his enthusiasm.

In that second home, so much more understanding than his own, James found in the younger Ernest Rousseau a true brother. When they were together they behaved almost childishly: Ernest would play the part of Pierrot (Ensor often portrayed him in the traditional costume), and James would play Fridolin. Pierrot specialized in pranks (*zwanze*, as the Brussels people called them) and grim jokes. Both young men were clever at dressing up and improvising charades. They wore masks when they took part in the Carnival, and often went to the circus together, one of James's sources of inspiration. – Fridolin would complain to Pierrot, who was a doctor, that he was losing his hair. Pierrot would then cover his face with a towel and vigorously rub in red ink. Fridolin had a panic fear of being ill. One day he was tired, and consulted Pierrot. The latter said: "I'll give you an excellent remedy, but I hope your urine won't change color; that would be a symptom of a deadly disease." Next day Fridolin's urine was bright blue: Pierrot had made him swallow some harmless, coloring matter. – Jokes followed pranks at the expense of one or the other, in turn, and involved not only friends, but total strangers.

The habitual atmosphere in the Rousseau home was one of high good spirits. Family and friends addressed one another with invented names, and acted out imaginary situations. Everyone joined in the games, catching on at once.

Ensor liked to study the insect collections of his friend, a passionate entomologist. He found in them a repertory of strange forms which he utilized in his own works.

In connection with Ernest's anatomical studies, bones and sometimes whole skeletons occasionally made their way into the Rousseau home; these, too, James used in his canvases, drawings, and etchings.

To be sure, if Ensor had not been a genius, the Rousseau milieu would not have made him one. Nevertheless, it is true that this milieu helped him to know himself and his genius, whereas in the heavy family atmosphere in Ostend his development might have been stunted.

GARDEN OF LOVE (detail, see c. c. 182). 1888

Too close acquaintance with the bizarre and the pathetic drives us now and again to value that which merely charms and relaxes, the spectacle of colors and forms saluting each other with perfect courtesy. Ensor liked, from time to time, to walk a little way down peaceful paths into enchanted flower gardens.

INTRIGUE (see details pp. 86, 87). 1890

An intricate mixture of coloristic subtleties, bizarre forms, futile gestures, latent uneasiness, making a fictitious drama of elusive passions, a mere pretext for the pleasure of painting. It is bathed in the captivating and poisonous light of Ensorian ambiguity. "Painting which is an expression of the painter's desires," as René Huyghe noted in his commentary to this picture, "may sometimes serve the opposite purpose of exorcising the demons that haunt him."

INTRIGUE (detail, see p. 85). 1890

INTRIGUE (detail, see p. 85). 1890

OLD WOMAN WITH MASKS (also called THE THEATER OF MASKS and BOUQUET D'ARTIFICE; detail, see c. c. 129). 1889

Unusually dense in tone, at once tired and glowing with life, disillusioned in expression, with a sickly smile and a vacant stare, "Old Woman with Masks" is a summing-up of Ensor's art. The work was commissioned as a portrait; the portrait did not please and the work was not accepted. Ensor repainted it for his own pleasure, making the elements that were disliked even more unpleasant. The mishap gave birth to a masterpiece.

THE DESPAIR OF PIERROT. 1892

This painting represents one of those imaginary situations that Ensor and his young friend Rousseau liked to create. In the center is the young Rousseau, in the costume of Pierrot, whom his father scolds for his debauchery and extravagance. The scene shows him mournfully regretting his excesses, saying only, "My father was right." He is surrounded by masks, images of those who have fleeced him. Closest to him is a moneylender with a hooked nose and on the extreme left a coarse procuress. Opposite her on the other side of the picture is the elder Rousseau, with a big mustache. Above him there is a servant who silently observes the scene. The background of the canvas is crammed with a number of more or less obvious allusions. Harlequin is taking Colombine away from Pierrot. At the upper left edge Ensor's sister, in profile, in a Salvation Army uniform, sermonizes and jeers. Under her, the young Rousseau, in his surgeon's uniform, tries to extract the "stone of madness" from the skull of Ensor, whose face is distorted by the operation.

The pictorial qualities of this painting raise it far above the plane of the merely anecdotal. The arrangement of the figures in the foreground suggests the arc of a circle, and may symbolize the "wheel of fortune." Ensor liked this work, referring quite accurately to its "translucent porcelain tones." Characteristic of a technique rarely employed by Ensor, and borrowed from Pointillism, is the crosshatching which is treated with a freedom that is a far cry from orthodox Pointillism.

Ensor was eager to exhibit his works, but this proved difficult. He was mistrusted everywhere, and the works he submitted for exhibition were as a rule rejected. A few canvases made their way into La Chrysalide, a group which also exhibited works by Rops, Dubois, Artan, Vogels, and Pantazis. The avant-garde group L'Essor tolerated his *Lamp Boy* (p. 33), but rejected his *Woman Eating Oysters* (p. 256), which was also refused by the Antwerp Salon. On one occasion, every one of his entries, including *Afternoon at Ostend* (pp. 53, 55), was rejected by the Brussels Salon.

However, a spirit of rebellion was brewing among a number of painters, writers, and other artists. Magazines like *La Jeune Belgique* and *L'Art Moderne* were founded, championing the new spirit, and Octave Maus took the initiative of creating Les XX (The Twenty), a society which gathered together the new painters in Belgium. In the course of the next ten to twenty years, the works of all the European *avant-garde* artists of the period, and especially the French ones, were introduced by that society – music from Wagner to Ravel, poetry from Villiers-de-l'Isle-Adam to Verlaine, and painting from Manet to Seurat and Toorop. According to the historian of modern art, Alfred H. Barr, Jr., Director of the Museum Collections of the Museum of Modern Art in New York City, Les XX was "at that time the most progressive art society in the world."

Ensor, though one of the founding members of Les XX was mistrusted there. Many *vingtistes* found his presence embarrassing to them, and his canvases were sometimes rejected even by his colleagues in that society. In 1888, every one of his entries was rejected. When he submitted his *Fall of the Rebellious Angels* (p. 79) and *The Entry of Christ into Brussels* (pp. 181, 274, 275), criticism changed to open hostility. The sculptor Achille Chainaye declared that he would resign from the group if Ensor remained. The question was put to a vote. Two ballots were taken, and Ensor barely escaped expulsion, thanks only to his own vote – for he was determined not to lose the only opportunity he had to show his work. As for the discourteous and not too perspicacious Chainaye, he was advantageously replaced by Auguste Rodin.

The founder of Les XX, Octave Maus, whom Ensor called "the Mandarin," had no love for the native of Ostend. This unfriendly fellow member held that Ensor had been ill-inspired to drop his "realistic" manner. If he had to develop, why couldn't he take the path of Plein-airism, Impressionism, or Pointillism, movements which met Maus's full approval? Why had he taken up a baffling, whimsical, and chaotic style, the provoking manner of a naughty boy? No doubt Maus was not alone in thinking this; some sound, very sound men shared his views less openly. Ensor reveals this fact when he teasingly makes Camille Lemonnier say: "We've done everything, Maus, Picard, and I, etc. etc. to keep this mulish Englishman in peasant shoes inside the rich, ripe compost pile of our fine Flemish painting.... But he always goes off on his own, and remains unclassifiable."

We cannot say whether his comrades and friends of the "somber" period – Dubois, Artan, Vogels, Finch, Pantazis, and the moderate revolutionaries of La Chrysalide – did or did not approve his giving up the first manner and plunging unexpectedly into fantasy. Some of them had died, others had left Belgium. As for those in whom it is possible to detect a direct though momentary influence by Ensor – Khnopff, Toorop, Van Strijdonck, and Charlet – they reflect only the Ensor of the middle-class interiors. There is every reason to believe that while some of his fellow painters had confidence in him as a friend, no one wholeheartedly approved the new direction his art had taken. Behind his back, his friends probably whispered that he was on the wrong track.

"The splendid song of art is infinitely varied . . . . Everything is a matter for painting, everything is good enough to be painted, everything is beautiful enough to be painted." Ensor practiced diversity as a system of expression. He turned against all those who clung to one formula, who continually repeated themselves, painting and repainting the same picture over and over again: "I pity painters who paint in a set style, who are doomed to produce uniform work in imitation of known models, for they outlaw the possibility of development. Deprived of the joys of discovery, shriveled-up fearfully inside their shells, mechanical machines for identical reproduction, servile hands and imaginations, closed to all effort, doomed to the sterility of facile elegance, pursuing it untiringly with neither advances nor retreats, stillborn, caught in their own trap." And elsewhere he says: "The narrow-minded want you forever to be beginning again, to keep going along the same track. They want the painter to paint his little works over and over again, and they condemn everything that goes further. That is how the minds of certain censors work, who label and classify our artists as though they were oysters neatly planted in beds."

As for himself, he deliberately defied the shortsighted critics who wanted to confine the painter to a single style of artistic expression – and this revolutionary attitude, which is essentially modern, was one of the reasons why he was ostracized by the artistic community. He wanted to be diverse, Protean, elusive. He seems to have heeded the advice given by Marcel Schwob: "Let us surrender to the universal law of dispersal." He wanted to take up all styles, all subjects, all feelings, all techniques. According to mood, he was in turn Realist, Naturalist, Impressionist, Symbolist, Pointillist, Fauve, Expressionist, Surrealist, and he was each of these irreverently, in no orthodox spirit, upsetting all classifications. As his whim dictated, under the impact of the emotion of the moment, but always with premeditation – for he never lost self-control – he would be arrogant, irresponsible, harsh, relaxed, admiring, affable, burlesque, exaggerated, embarrassing. And each time he adopted or invented the style, the exact pictorial vocabulary that matched his state of mind – his failures are rare. Now he would lay on the paint with a trowel, and now he would imitate a Japanese master, now he would lightly caress the canvas, and now he would set down each form with harsh insistence.

In a spirit of intellectual playfulness, of sheer bravado, enjoying experiment for its own sake, he would even take pleasure in plagiarizing, in transmuting himself into Courbet, Hokusai, De Braekeleer, Rembrandt, Watteau, Bosch, Turner, Manet, Bruegel, into a Sunday painter, a sidewalk painter, an apocalyptic painter, and while he was at it, a Bonnard before Bonnard, a Dufy before Dufy.

His borrowings and plagiarisms were deliberate; if they had been unconscious, as happens to so many proud or innocent plagiarists, they would have made him ridiculous or foolish. But Ensor, fully aware of what he was doing, offers rare delicacies to the gourmets of painting, delicacies flavored with technical refinements, and delightfully seasoned with humor.

Being a constitutive element of his art, Ensor's diversity paradoxically became one of the elements that assured its coherence. Comprehending the multiple led to unity, a unity that seemed continually in jeopardy, but that was in fact discreetly present under the delectable variety.

ATTRIBUTES OF THE STUDIO. 1889

ART AS PLAY

Surely, all art is a game, the creation of a fictitious universe to replace the real world that is too humdrum, both inaccessible and too accessible. No art is more clearly a game than Ensor's. Whereas Leonardo is the type of *homo sapiens*, the cerebral and calculating artist, and Vermeer the type of *homo faber*, the sensual and craftsmanlike artist, Ensor is the type of *homo ludens*, the imaginative and whimsical artist. His orientation toward the invented, the gratuitous, the fictitious, the playful in the broadest sense, is obvious. In this he is not alone: Lucas van Leyden, Alessandro Magnasco, Henri Rousseau are similarly oriented. But no other artist is equally accomplished as *homo ludens*, given so completely, and it would seem, exclusively, to all forms of playful activity. No other artist derives all his behavior, his mode of expression, and, in so far as he has one, his philosophy, from play. The idea of play is doubtless the golden key that opens the door to a deeper understanding of this painter-conjurer, of this master of the puzzling.

Play, whether the play of children, of primitives, or of poets, whether mere amusement or sacred rite, derives originally – according to Huizinga and other psychologists – from the rejection of everyday life. It serves as an escape from reality, from the ordinary commandments and prohibitions. It observes its own laws, different from those of everyday existence; it constitutes a voluntary withdrawal into a fictitious situation; it substitutes inconsequential seriousness for a seriousness heavy with consequences; it is free activity, gratifying the need for relaxation and gratuitousness, providing a joyful outlet for excess vitality. Through the fictions of play we gratify desires that cannot be gratified in real life. We find the occasion for experiencing extreme tensions, enthusiasm, and raptures. Play is often alienation through imitation, disguise, fabulation, or distortion; frequently it resorts to the "as if," which suggests reality without assuming it. By simulating reality it makes possible acts of transcendence impossible in nonplayful situations, an indefinite multiplication of the self, which makes up for the inadequacy of one's personal life, giving access to diversity, to the universal, to that which Suzanne Lilar, subtle expounder of analogism, calls "illimitation." But in the back of the mind of him who plays there persists a certain awareness of the unreality of it all ("I know that I'm deluding myself, but I want to delude myself, and take my delusions seriously") which both encourages him to be daring and makes his play harmless, thus, in the end, humanizing it.

All these characteristics of play apply also to Ensor, to his artistic conceptions, to his attitude toward life.

He escaped into his art, he confined himself in it as the player within his "field of play." Ordinary existence became alien to him (he might have said with Mallarmé, "I run away and keep my face pressed against the window panes, turning my back to life" or, with Charles Cros, "I live outside my own life"). He dodged all real commitments, adhering to no party, to no aesthetic formula, to no religion, shunning travel, marriage, paternity. With Huysmans' hero Des Esseintes he seemed to believe: "Why go out, since I can make such splendid trips without leaving my chair." Thus he put himself outside of good and evil, outside life's "dreary laws." He turned inward, he "escaped" without going anywhere. In his inner refuge he felt free, and indulged in every daring venture, and like the authentic great poet he was, gave himself up to his games with wild enthusiasm, like a child playing ball, like a savage playing witch doctor. He was the more daring in his fictitious life because he refused to be daring in real life.

In the realm of play, the timid and the imaginative in Ensor's make-up found compensation. Like all passionate gamblers, he took his games seriously, and defended them tooth and nail. He forgot everyday life; his true life, in the last analysis, was art. For only in imagination could he live intensely and break through the habitual limits. Hence his tendency to paint *as if* he were Rembrandt, or Turner, or Teniers – his fondness for masks and disguises, which is another sign of repressed timidity, and another occasion for increasing the number of possible selves. Hence also his eagerness to try all subjects, all techniques, all styles, all emotions, to participate,

from his prison, in the great universal game. He had a passion for all kinds of play –
inoffensive puns and caricatures; the play of wit and the play of light; plays on form
and technique; carnival pranks, grimaces, theater; games of anger and indignation;
imaginary combats and murders; cosmic upheavals and social revolutions; the great
games of history, religion, and annihilation.

HYMNS TO LIGHT

Ensor, who was close to seeing logical reason as a mortal danger to art, continually
sought stimulants for his poetic digressions in the digressions of nature. The people
of Ostend often saw the tall, thin silhouette of the painter striding along the beach or
roaming the dunes, accompanied by two pug dogs chasing each other, barking,
running into the surf and out again, or rolling in the sand.

Light and the sea, Ostend's capricious royal presences, were Ensor's great friends.
He composed brief but passionate odes to light: "Light is my daughter, Light the
one and indivisible, Light the painter's bread, Light the Queen of our senses. Light,
Light, enlighten us! Inspire us, show us new ways to joy and happiness!" To him
impalpable light was made flesh: "The goddess of painting holds me close in her
iridescent arms. She shows me the importance of light, I might say the form of light,
the structure of light." Painting and light become indistinguishable: "What painting
says to me is: sun, sky, daylight, light, always light." Such remarks invite us to
regard his art, from the first attempts to its highest realizations, as a sequence of
variations on the single theme of light. If this were so, Ensor's art would have to be
classified under Impressionism, but as an Impressionism of a superior kind, which,

like that of Cézanne and Van Gogh, transcends Impressionism. This is a tempting thesis. It suggests that Ensor's light is both of the physical and the spiritual order, that it reveals both the tangible and the intangible, matter and the dream, providing the painter with a mental palette of colors: the sullen light of the middle-class interiors; the cheerful light of *Ostend Rooftops* (p. 67) with their clear skies; flashes of lightning in storms and scenes of terror; the shimmering light of the sea; the light of beaches and gardens; the light diffused by colors; the light of a Kôrín or of a Turner; the light emanating from masks; the light of a Christ and the lights of hell; the fairy lights and the light of dreams. Each variation, each statement of light, is for Ensor a springboard to endless analogy.

Some canvases – *Fall of the Rebellious Angels* (p. 79), *The Domain of Arnheim* (c.c. 66), *Adam and Eve Driven from Paradise* or *Study of Light* (p. 241) – are nothing but streams of light, in which all the forms, all the subjects are drowned. They forecast the exacerbated Impressionism that Monet was to practice ten or fifteen years later, when he painted the series of the Rouen cathedral, and of the Nymphéas. The same lyrical vision of light make the Ostend and the Vétheuil painters alike, precursors of the "warm" or romantic school of non-figurative art. And yet Ensor – by virtue of his secondary, tertiary, and even remoter intentions, of an ideological, imaginative, and even, in this case, mystical order – eludes not only the aesthetics of abstraction, but also Impressionism.

CARNIVAL ON THE BEACH. 1887

Here we have a subtle interplay between technique and subject, which complement each other. The subtleties of the treatment, the mist-laden light, beget dreamlike figures in the manner of Watteau. One thinks of some embarkation for Cythera that has been interrupted, the pilgrims of joy deciding not to go on with their journey but staying where they are, ravished with the charm of the place and the gentleness of the light.

CHRIST CALMING THE WATERS. 1891

Ensor treated this subject several times; the initial version was one of his earliest etchings. Although Ensor's works are never religious in the conventional sense, they represent Christ as an exceptional figure whose moral strength prevails over the violence of human passions and the elements of nature. To Ensor, these elements often symbolize unleashed passions.

PAINTER OF THE SEA

Ensor's lasting affection for Ostend primarily reflected his love for the sea. According to Joseph Muls, "It was the ocean, the North Sea, that fashioned Ensor's soul. His lungs were filled from the very first with the breath of the sea. His eyes plumbed the endless marine horizons. It is the sea that gives such unusual luminosity to his canvases." Ensor himself tells us what he owed to the sea: "I gaze for long periods at the comforting sea, at its problematic colors and the perpetual somersaults of the curling waves, always straightening themselves out again. I study its varied aspects, its clouded forms, its opalescent, milky atmosphere." He sang its virtues in no uncertain terms: "Medicinal sea, worshiped Mother, I should like to offer one fresh, simple bouquet celebrating your hundred faces, your surfaces, your facets, your dimples, your rubescent underparts, your diamond-studded crests, your sapphire overlay, your blessings, your delights, your deep charms." He speaks of it as a beloved woman: "Night and morning I give her long embraces. Ah! my beloved sea's good kisses, sublimated kisses, perfumed with foam, tangy, bracing." The sea gives him aid and comfort: "Pure sea, inspirer of energy and steadfastness.... Yes, I owe a great deal to the sea!" It has something to teach him: "Let us be great and deep like the sea."

Intrigued and amused, Ensor depicted everything that his "great inspirer" holds, bears upon itself, rejects, draws to itself, or suggests. He loved it under all its aspects and at all times – silvery and misty as Artan saw it, laughing as Spilliaert was to see it, and heavy and oily as Permeke would see it. He joyfully welcomed the teeming life of its coasts and broad surface – ships, fishermen, fishwives, bathers, and all the strange beings begotten of its conjunctions with air, sand, and the fiery sun: mermaids with seaweed hair, ballerinas in tutus of spume, Christs calming the waters, and demons unleashing storms.

He cast his nets deep and pulled them out heavy with queer shells, grimacing fish – flat as leaves or long as snakes – crustaceans, the flotsam of sunken ships, skeletons, monsters and divinities of the sea: in short, a madder, more bizarre Carnival than the one that sweeps through the streets of Ostend at Mid-Lent.

And yet this painter of the sea is not a seascapist. He gives us many far-fetched interpretations of the sea, suggesting its vastness, its contortions, its moods, and its spirit; he makes a sea of his *Battle of the Golden Spurs* (p. 123, c.c. 157), his *Entry of Christ into Brussels* (pp. 181, 274, 275), his *Carnival on the Beach* (p. 103), yet only rarely does he represent it directly. His seascapes are of minor importance in his work as a whole.

BOATS ON THE BEACH. About 1892

Ensor made an etching of the same subject in 1888 (see p. 112). He painted it again in 1900, using a very different treatment of more sharply contrasting tones, with brown dominating (see p. 273).

SKILLFUL MIXTURES

Ensor often liked to juxtapose and weld together the different elements of his art, and the various styles he used. He deliberately encouraged confusion. The pictures he sent to exhibitions were heterogeneous; he liked to group realistic works with more imaginative ones, the idyllic and the grotesque side by side; in his opinion each complemented the other. In his studio, he was accustomed to work simultaneously on canvases of diametrically opposed styles. When he set out on a new work, he often resorted to one of his earlier manners. But he often also introduced seemingly ill-matched elements into the same work, in which he would harmonize them, and thus endow it with multiple aspects and echoes.

The impression of complexity suggested by most of his works is not deceptive; to talk with Ensor would confirm this, and to read his writings would prove it. He intended that the sands of his pictures should turn into bathers; he intended that the sea water should become shells or petals; and he intended that the shimmering air should also appear to us as saved or fallen angels. He organizes vast rearrangements. Sky, earth, and water are linked, are separated, are juxtaposed. Fishes, vegetables, game, and flowers hold common converse. Archangels, tramps, and mermaids call out to each other.

Ensor himself is a mixture of painter, writer, and musician. His brushes are violin bows, his pen a reed pipe. His musical notes are colors, his colors are words, and his words are musical notes. According to him, painting is the collective work of all the senses, touch, smell, hearing, sight: "Yes, all the senses take part in the sacred pleasure; first the eye, then the taste, then the touch; finally, the mind, whose essence is humbler."

It has often been said that Ensor's complexity is accounted for by his mixed parentage. His father was English, his mother was Flemish with a Spanish strain on her mother's side. It is certain that Ensor shows affinities with the Englishmen Rowlandson, Hogarth, Turner, and Beardsley, with the Flemings Bosch, Bruegel, and Teniers, and with the Spaniards Goya and Picasso. His verve is Flemish, his phlegm British, his restlessness Spanish. But such qualities, while characteristic of certain nations, are also universal, in the sense that we find them in some individuals at all times and all places.

TARGET OF ABUSE

While Ensor was advancing boldly and exultantly from discovery to discovery, and his painter friends at least tolerated him, permitting him to show the products of his strenuous efforts at the Salon of Les XX, the critics were heaping contempt on him. They had a poor enough opinion of Les XX on the whole, but it was Ensor, the most independent member of the group, whom they singled out for particularly savage attacks.

The reviewer of *Le Courier Belge*, after his visit to one of the annual Salons of Les XX, described it as "an exhibition by practical jokers, who have only contempt for the public, art, good taste, and good manners." The reviewer of *High-Life* reassured his distinguished readers: "Faithful to their tradition, Les XX have invited Belgian and foreign artists . . . including such humbugs as Seurat and Pissarro. Such innovators are not taken seriously by any artist, and do not deserve to be." Renoir was attacked: "One glance is enough to see the poverty of his flashy palette." Referring to Van Gogh, the reviewer of *L'Eventail* was more determined to play it safe: "If I told you that I accept for a moment the carnival art of Vincent van Gogh, you wouldn't believe it!" An article devoted to the Salon of 1891 in *Le Conservateur* sums up the results of several years' of the group's activity: "This exhibition is no less grotesque than the preceding ones." According to the writer, the group was composed of neurotics and humbugs: "It is as though one were to sit down in the midst of a circus or Mardi Gras."

Ensor had to cope with this attitude by the critics ever since 1881: "The very first time I exhibited, at La Chrysalide, although my intentions were peaceful, I upset pictorial convention. The critics vied with each other in tearing me to pieces .... I was abused, insulted, proclaimed a madman, a fool; I was called nasty, bad, incapable, and ignorant. A simple cabbage somehow became obscene; my placid interiors, my bourgeois salons, hotbeds of revolution." When he began to show with Les XX, "the critics multiplied their attacks, the most savage blows being exchanged with passion. For ten years they snarled without let-up, strangled without mercy."

Ensor was the chief target of the abuse and the jeers. *Mission de l'Art* set the tone: "One is nauseated at the disgusting performances of the various Ensors, Monets, Seurats, and Gauguins, who, under pretext of artistic freedom, put frames around the most disgusting studio garbage .... To admire, with equal admiration, the sinister idiocy of an Ensor and the suave plasticity of a Burne-Jones, is to discredit the proud sentiment of beauty, to lower it to a culpable bad taste." Max Sulzberger, forgotten today, but very influential at the time, went one better: "We have seen mediocre exhibitions before this, but we never imagined that aberration on the part of the fanatics of novelty would attain this pitch of insanity, not to say ignominy." A muddled painter who published reviews signed "Un artiste," took up his pen and ironized: "As for Monsieur Ensor, it is quite clear that he suffers from some disease of the eyes .... It is as though he rubbed his pictures one against the other – on the painted side – before they were dry. This would account for the fact that in his *Afternoon at Ostend* (pp. 53, 55) a bit of the lady's dress spills over onto her face, that some of her face is on her hat, and that her hat has spilled over onto the mantlepiece." *L'Etoile Belge* was dismayed: "In striking contrast with everything anyone has ever seen before, M. James Ensor exhibits a series of formless studies, painful in appearance, and sad to behold. – The men and women he paints, as he paints them, are incapable of movement, while the inanimate objects execute crazy sarabands and are always off balance." Gustave Lagye exclaims: "What is the point of putting such jokes on exhibit?" His fellow critic Champal was in despair: "This time, with tears in my eyes, I give up!" "They are not paintings, not even sketches – just daubings!" said the *Gazette* in 1886. The same line was taken by *Le Patriote* in 1894: "You call this painting? Come, come! It's garbage!"

Ensor, entirely absorbed in his work, was not distracted. The criticism and the abuse made him suffer, sometimes to the point of tears, but thanks to his talent and his irony he was able to forget his bitter disappointment. And we may surmise that he was also sustained by the secret joy which is that of the precursor, aware that he was making important innovations. The fact that he was not understood mattered little: he knew that his work was valid, despite everything.

ENSOR AND GENERAL LEMAN DISCUSSING PAINTING. 1890

At the center, listening to the debate, Mariette Rousseau. At the Rousseaus, Ensor had frequent and violent quarrels about art with General Leman, future defender of the Liége fortress in 1914. (There is an excellent copy of this panel, made by Ensor himself.)

Boats on the Beach. 1888

MASTER ENGRAVER

Ensor would be regarded as a great master, an exceptional and complete artist, even if only his engravings were known. Moreover, he would be looked upon as another Callot, another Piranese, another Posada, rather than another Gustave Doré or Gavarni. Unlike many painters who have occasionally made etchings, he was a painter who was also a fully accomplished etcher, like Dürer or Goya. Among his contemporaries from Manet to Bonnard, the only artist who was at all comparable to him in this respect was Odilon Redon, who also seems to have expressed his full genius in etchings.

The Cathedral – Die Kathedrale – La cattedrale (1886)

Portrait of Ernest Rousseau – Portrait Ernest Rousseau – Ritratto di Ernest Rousseau (1887)

Ostend Docks – Docks in Ostende – Pontile a Ostenda (1887)

The Great Basin at Ostend – Das große Hafenbecken von Ostende – Il grande bacino di Ostenda (1888)

Woods at Groenendael – Gehölz bei Groenendael – Sottobosco a Groenendael (1888)

Grove – Das Wäldchen – Gruppo d'alberi (1888)

Kermess at the Windmill – Kirmes bei der Windmühle – La kermesse al mulino (1889)

Skull and Masks – Schädel und Masken – Crani e maschere (1888)
Odd Insects – Seltsame Insekten – Strani insetti (1888)

Murder – Der Mord – L'assassinio (1888)
Gendarmes – Die Gendarmen – I gendarmi (1888)

Devils' Sabbath – Teufel auf dem Wege zum Sabbat – Diavoli che si recano al Sabbat (1887)
Combat of Demons – Dämonenkampf – Combattimento di diavoli (1888)

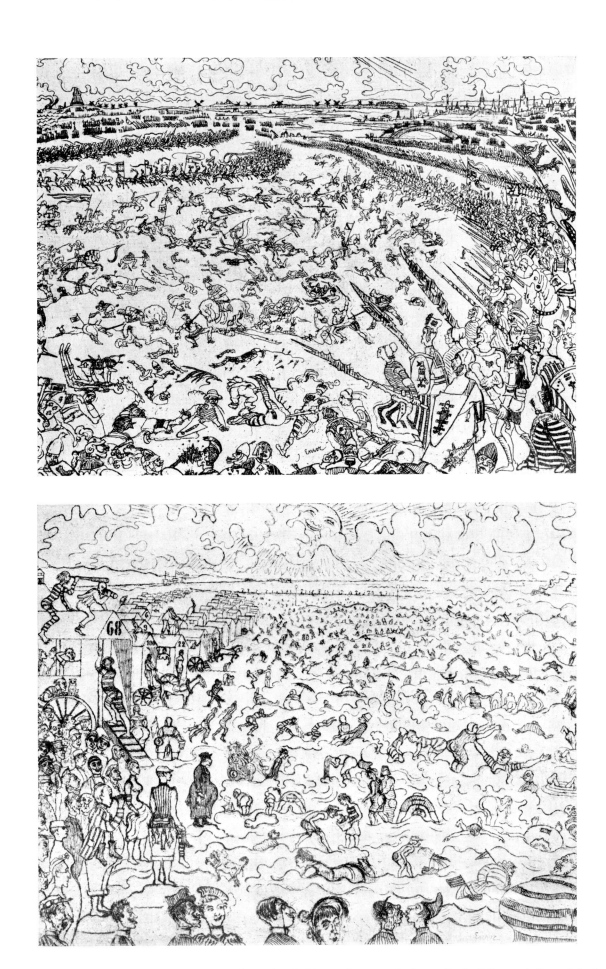

The Battle of the Golden Spurs – Die Schlacht der Goldenen Sporen – La battaglia degli Speroni d'oro (1895)
Beach at Ostend – Der Strand von Ostende – I bagni di Ostenda (1899)

Gamblers – Die Spieler – I giocatori
(1895)

Demons Tormenting Me – Dämonen,
die mich quälen – Diavoli che mi beffano
(1895)

Napoleon's Farewell – Napoleons Ab-
schied – L'addio di Napoleone (1897)

Christ Tormented by Demons
Christus, von Dämonen gequält
Cristo tormentato dai diavoli (1895)

Christ Among the Beggars – Christus
und die Bettler – Il Cristo dei mendi-
canti (1895)

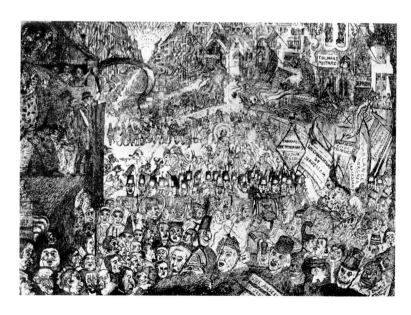

The Entry of Christ into Brussels
Christi Einzug in Brüssel
L'ingresso di Cristo a Bruxelles
(1898)

Combat – Der Kampf – Il combattimento (1896)

Scandalized Masks – Verärgerte Masken
Le maschere scandalizzate (1895)

Lady Godiva (1933)

Triumph of Death – Der Triumph des Todes – Il trionfo della Morte (1896)

The Vengeance of Hop Frog – Hop Frogs Rache – La vendetta di Hop Frog (1898)

Ensor's graphic oeuvre comprises a total of 133 prints, most of them executed during two particularly fruitful periods, one between 1886 and 1889, and the other between 1895 and 1899. With his very first plate he showed himself a master of the technique; the very first year he took up etching, he produced masterpieces. He explored this new field thoroughly, with restless curiosity and intense pleasure in discovery. As he did also in the case of painting, he practiced all the types of etching simultaneously, putting works aside and coming back to them intermittently. A classification by type is possible only if we disregard chronology.

Of the portraits in realistic style, among which are one of himself, one of the botanist Frise, and one of the Socialist leader Hector Denis, the best is that of his friend Ernest Rousseau (p. 114), firmly delineated and striking in its physical and psychological truth: crowning the ample black surface of the garment, the massive face expresses calm forcefulness, in which insight and kindness are also evident. This portrait represents one of the extremes of Ensor's etching, a solid realism; at the other extreme we find an unrestrained lyricism. Between the two is a range of varied artistic expressions. There is the series of landscapes, such as *Wind* (c. c. 65) and *Pond with Poplars* (c. c. 63), vibrant with mysterious life, the foliage throbbing with light; there are the gentle or emotion-laden seascapes, such as *Boats on the Beach* (p. 112) or *Christ Calming the Waters*; the extremely personal views of Brussels, Ostend, and Oudenaerde; the peaceful lunar gardens of love; the deliberate imitations of Rembrandt, Titian, Michelangelo, Claude Lorrain, and others, which gave birth to the subtle poetry of *Render unto Caesar*, and the heavy atmosphere of *Celebrated Persian Physicians;* the satires and burlesque evocations; the visions of absurdity and death such as *Odd Insects* (p. 118) or *My Portrait in 1960* (p. 206; see also c. c. 25); the scenes showing devils invading the skies or the bowels of the earth; and finally, the large lyrical compositions, such as *The Vengeance of Hop Frog* (p. 128), *Capture of a Strange City* (p. 120), *Triumph of Death* (p. 127), and *The Cathedral* (p. 113), of such astonishing technical skill and epic scale as to be unforgettable.

A continual spirit of invention present in all these works kept Ensor's engraving from ever bogging down into formula. With his copper or zinc plates before him,

Ensor chose, according to the subject he intended to treat, the nature of his drawing, the treatment, the kind of acid or inking – he planned them in advance – that seemed to him the most suitable. The sureness of his choice, the masterful manner in which he carried out his work, give most of his plates a quality of improvisation and lack of constraint, which largely account for their charm. Precision and imprecision are skillfully blended. The line may be incisive or hesitant, pricking or caressing, sinuous or curly. According to the nature of the scene represented, the lighting is gentle, vaporous, downy, sparkling, flashing, more rarely cold or arrogant. Even colors are evoked: sensations of color variations are suggested by means of certain technical subtleties. The style, too, varies: sometimes it is deliberately tortured in the Pre-Raphaelite manner, sometimes carefree, heralding Surrealism; most often it lovingly follows all the modulations of an unorthodox Impressionism. In the last analysis, it is the composition that serves as Ensor's principal means of expression in his etchings. By means of it, by opening up perspectives, organizing skies, conducting crowds, building cities, he succeeds in endowing some of his plates, frequently of quite modest dimensions, with uncommon grandeur, with a kind of cosmic quality.

FIGURES. 1880

There are many sketches and preliminary studies in pencil, ink, and watercolor that Ensor accumulated in preparing more important works, or made merely for the pleasure of recording things. They are intensely animated, which is all the more striking because the means used are reduced to a minimum.

DRAWINGS, WATERCOLORS, AND CHARCOALS

Everywhere and at all times, at school, at home with his family, on visits to museums, in the company of friends, while staying with the Rousseaus, taking walks, in his letters, Ensor made drawings. He drew in ink, with *crayons*, with watercolor, with red chalk, with charcoal. He usually carried a sketchbook with him, but when he had none, any scrap of paper he could lay his hands on was good enough – blank pages in a book, backs of envelopes, margins of a letter or of a program, or, if need be, an old drawing that had not taken up the entire space. Occasionally he made different drawings, in radically different styles, one on top of the other. He obviously enjoyed such effects of accident and surprise, so very much in what we might call the "Ensorian" spint. Enchanted by them, he carried both just a little short of founding an aesthetic system upon them. Executed in this spirit are many strangely poetic yet realistic drawings, done entirely in chiaroscuro or in velvety tones, over which it amused Ensor to trace characters, gestures, and expressions solely of his imagination, generally in a linear style.

Sometimes this expansion of the ordinary limits of drawing took another direction. One sheet of paper having been filled, Ensor would take another one, put it next to the first and continue his drawing on the second sheet. Thus, several sheets might be added to the first, surrounding it on both sides, at the top and below, as the drawing kept on growing. One *Temptation of St. Anthony* was done this way. Very large in size, it is composed of several juxtaposed sheets, each covered with number-less figures.

Whether representing sailors, fishermen, or devils, humble objects or biblical scenes, portraits (often of himself, with disquieting glance) or satirical scenes, studies of old masters, or sketches for pictures that may or may not have been painted, Ensor's drawings assay the most varied subjects in the most disparate styles, but we feel that all of them emanate from a solidly centered, anything but scattered, mind.

The complete list of this treasure of little-known drawings, many of them unpub-lished, remains to be drawn up. More than any other aspect of his art, his drawings illuminate for us the workings of his mind and his methods of creation.

Old Horse – Altes Pferd – Il vecchio cavallo (1880)

Sailboat, after Turner – Segelschiff, nach Turner – Barca a vela, da Turner (c. 1877)

1

2

3

1

Woman at a Café Table, after Degas – Frau im Café, nach Degas – Donna al caffè, da Degas (c. 1885)

2

Old Woman with Other Figures, after Rembrandt
Alte Frau, von Gestalten umgeben, nach Rembrandt
Vecchia attorniata da figure, da Rembrandt (c. 1878)

3

Silhouette of an Incroyable, after Grévin
Silhouette einer »Incroyable«, nach Grévin
Figura di «incroyable», da Grévin (c. 1885)

4

Chinoiserie – Chinoiserie – Cineserie (1885)

5

Grotesque Figure, after Daumier – Groteske Figur, nach Daumier – Figura grottesca, da Daumier (c. 1885)

4

5

Silhouettes – Silhouetten – Figure (1880)
Silhouettes – Silhouetten – Figure (c. 1880)

Silhouettes – Silhouetten – Figure (1880)
Silhouettes – Silhouetten – Figure (1880)

Young Sailor, Ostend – Ostender Schiffsjunge
Mozzo di Ostenda (1880)

Study – Studie – Studio (c. 1880)

The Guitarist – Der Gitarrenspieler – Il chitarrista
(1888)

Portrait of a Man – Männliches Portrait – Ritratto
maschile (1880)

The Musicians – Musikanten – I musicanti (1880)

Man with a Pan – Mann mit Topf – Uomo con la pentola
(1880)

Young Woman Seated – Sitzende junge Frau – Giovane
donna seduta (1880)

1

2

Lamp – Lampe – Lampada (c. 1881)

Attributes of the Studio – Atelierzubehör – Accessori
dello studio (c. 1882)

1

Glass – Glas – Bicchiere (1882)

2

Glasses – Gläser – Bicchieri (c. 1882)

Burlesque Figures – Burleske Figuren – Figure
burlesche (c. 1880)

Figures – Figuren – Figure (c. 1880)   Draught Horses – Zugpferde – Cavalli da tiro (c. 1880)

Writing Woman – Schreibende Frau – Donna che scrive
(1883)

Self-Portrait – Selbstportrait – Autoritratto (c. 1885)

Ensor and His Family – Ensor und seine Familie – Ensor e la sua famiglia (1886)

Woman Sewing – Nähende Frau – Donna che cuce (1881)

Haunted Mantlepiece – Der Kaminspuk – Il caminetto stregato (1885)

Portrait of My Mother – Das Portrait meiner Mutter – Ritratto di mia madre (c. 1885)

The Descent from the Cross – Die Kreuzabnahme – La discesa dalla croce (1886)

The Raising of the Cross – Die Aufrichtung des Kreuzes – L'innalzamento sulla croce (1913)

King Pest – König Pest – Il re Peste (1880)

Futurist Dream – Der Zukunftstraum – Sogno futurista (1886)

The Devil in the Belfry – Der Teufel im Glockenturm – Il diavolo nel campanile (c. 1888)

Carnival at Brussels – Karneval in Brüssel – Carnevale a Bruxelles (1888)

Hail Jesus, King of the Jews – Heil dir, Jesus, König der Juden – Salve Gesù, re dei Giudei (1885)

Christ Driving the Money Changers from the Temple
Vertreibung der Wechsler aus dem Tempel
Cristo scaccia i mercanti dal tempio (1886)

Christ in Agony – Der sterbende Christus – Cristo morente (1888)

The Sermon of St. Babilas – Die Predigt
des heiligen Salbadrius – La predica di San
Babila (1892)

Belgium in the Nineteenth Century – Belgien im neunzehnten Jahrhundert – Il Belgio nel XIX secolo (c. 1889)

Decadent Romans – Römer der Verfallszeit – Romani della decadenza (c. 1920)

Cathedral – Die Kathedrale – La cattedrale (c. 1890)
Christ in Hell – Christus in der Hölle – Cristo all'inferno (1891)

Small Persian Torture
Kleine persische Tortur
Piccola tortura persiana
(1896)

Temptation of St. Anthony – Die Versuchung des heiligen Antonius – La tentazione di Sant'Antonio (c. 1905)

Infamous Vivisectors
Die niederträchtigen Vivisekteure
Gli infami vivisettori
(1925)

Madame Demolder as Toreador – Madame Demolder als Torero – La signora Demolder in costume da torero (1895)

Frolicking Walkyrias
Walkürenritt
Divertimenti di Valchirie
(c. 1905)

White and Red Clowns Evolving – Weiße und rote Clowns in Bewegung – Pagliacci bianchi e rossi in movimento
(1890)

The Deadly Sins – Die Todsünden – I Peccati capitali (1902)

Gluttony – Die Völlerei – La gola

Anger – Der Zorn – L'ira

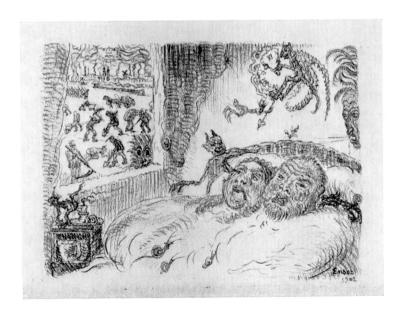

Sloth – Die Trägheit – L'accidia

Avarice – Der Geiz – L'avarizia

Pride – Der Hochmut – La superbia

Lust – Die Wollust – La lussuria

The Cook at the Billiard Table – Der Koch am Billard – Il cuoco al biliardo (1903)

Henri De Groux at the Billiard Table – Henri De Groux am Billard – Henri De Groux al biliardo (1907)

Louis XIV at the Billiard Table – Louis XIV. am Billard Luigi XIV al biliardo (1903)

Napoleon at the Billiard Table – Napoleon am Billard Napoleone al biliardo (1903)

Drunks at the Billiard Table – Trinker am Billard Ubriaconi al biliardo (1903)

Hitting the Cloth – Der Stoß in das Billardtuch – Colpo di stecca nel panno del biliardo (1903)

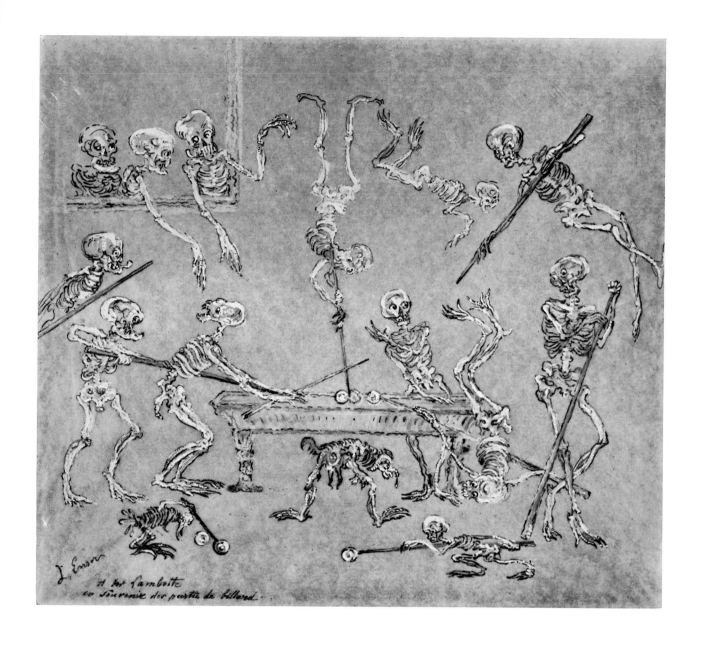

Skeletons Playing Billiards – Skelette am Billard
Scheletri al biliardo (1903)

Skeletons Playing Billiards – Skelette am Billard
Scheletri al biliardo (1903)

Self-Portrait – Selbstportrait – Autoritratto (c. 1940)

PAINTER OF MASKS

One of the many original seeds that Ensor scattered so prodigally was destined to take root and spread over almost the entire field of his art. In 1879, the very first year that, with his self-portraits, he proved he was a painter, he executed a small painting, *Mask Gazing at a Negro Mountebank*, which is in itself of minor importance yet significant in that it contains the first of many masks. The idea of the mask was from that moment on to develop slowly, to grow and gain weight, to acquire multiple meanings – pictorial, psychological, and intellectual. In 1883, in the middle of his "somber" and realistic period, Ensor painted *Scandalized Masks* (p. 287), showing two figures drawn with obvious pleasure, but treated quite objectively, in the act of putting on masks (it was this same year that Ensor painted himself with a flowered hat on his head) and staring at each other flabbergasted. The encounter of these stares produced a spark, kindling a secret fire that continued to smoulder, and, a few years later, was to set off a conflagration, a whole carnival of masks. Then came a succession of major works. In five years, from 1887 to 1891, the art of painting was enriched by unexpected, unprecedented masterpieces, of total originality – *Carnival on the Beach* (p. 103), *Masks Confronting Death* (p. 292), *The Entry of Christ into Brussels* (pp. 181, 274, 275), *Old Woman with Masks* (p. 89, c. c. 129), *Astonishment of the Mask Wouse* (p. 169), *Intrigue* (pp. 85, 86, 87), *Skeletons Fighting for the Body of a Hanged Man* (p. 175, c. c. 130). "I have joyously shut myself up in the solitary domain where the mask holds sway, wholly made up of violence, light, and brilliance," Ensor writes. "To me the mask means freshness of tone, acute expression, sumptuous decor, great unexpected gestures, unplanned movements, exquisite turbulence." By divesting the mask of all anecdotal features, he was able, while executing works of power and refinement, to give a playful, indirect, and strong expression to his colorful, sorrowful, and yet humorous vision of a world ruled by absurdity, where disconnected thoughts and futile actions rub shoulders with vicious and ridiculous passions.

In 1899, when he painted himself looking at us mockingly with eyes at once sad and questioning, he is wearing a buffoon's hat, but at the same time he is surrounded and assailed by a whole crowd of masks, each of which is a mockery in itself and a superb piece of painting (p.165).

It was a combination of external circumstances, artistic exploration and self-amusement, a deep need to escape from everyday life into play as well as a severe personal judgment of life, that induced Ensor to fix on the mask and to make of it a major mode of expression. Masks had been looking at him from childhood on in those family shops which were playrooms for him, and they had become for him dimly troubling, obsessive figures. At Carnival time (the Ostend Carnival is famous) he watched masks bobbing atop disguised bodies, often in tatters, taking on the disquieting appearance of ghosts, the oddly noble, unalterable aspect of a man in disguise. In the streets of Ostend, particularly at the famous ball of the Rat Mort he watched his fellow citizens, members of his family (especially his grandmother) dressing up in masquerade, turning themselves into different personalities – terrifying, queer, or grotesque – changing their age and their sex, transforming themselves into skeletons, animals, or objects of daily use, and taking on the most unpredictable appearances while somehow remaining themselves. He, too, accompanied by his faithful friend Ernest Rousseau (as Pierrot) would dress up and roam the streets of Ostend or Brussels, unrecognized, uttering animal cries, inventing strange gestures, delighted at the occasion to take off into the absurd. Under cover of the mask, he could indulge in the comforting, yet withal desperate, game of alienation.

By this time he had acquired a disabused knowledge of man; faces and expressions seemed to him means of camouflage for concealing hypocrisy, and he in his turn took pleasure in this camouflage, happy to increase the confusion, to put the cheaters-at-cards out of countenance by jumbling their stacked decks. He had also observed the great carnival of nature, of which the cardboard and tinsel carnivals are the image – the numberless monsters, both great and small, the fish and shells which dwell in the sea, lie stranded on the beaches, or are caught in fishermen's nets; the strange shapes of insects reproduced in his friend Pierrot's textbooks; the fantastic

PORTRAIT OF THE ARTIST SURROUNDED BY MASKS. 1899

In a caricature of Rubens, Ensor takes a perplexed and skeptical look at himself, surrounded by ridiculous cardboard faces that are expressing human passions. In much the same spirit, Bosch, one of Ensor's spiritual ancestors, represented Christ bearing the Cross as overwhelmed by sadness and throbbing with lucidity in the midst of cruel and grimacing faces of flesh.

forms of the plants and cells in Mariette Rousseau's herbarium and mounted on her microscope slides.

Thus Ensor discovered in the folly of the mask, as in the follies of nature, an untapped mine of the pictorial, a possibility of employing form with increased freedom: "Oh, the animal masks of the Ostend Carnival: bloated vicuna faces, misshapen birds with the tails of birds of paradise, cranes with sky-blue bills gabbling nonsense, obtuse sciolists with moldy skulls, peculiar insects, hard shells giving shelter to soft beasts." The Ostend Carnival, on the frontier between reality and unreality, became the very image of the human, the universal carnival.

Answering an ambiguous need to destroy and extend the "self," the mask enabled Ensor to play a Pirandello game with the personality. Sometimes he turned the mask into a real face, at other times the real face becomes a mask. Vices, passions, and virtues are perhaps but masks concealing unknown, unknowable faces. While the truth alters, the disquiet that Ensor has astutely set in motion, spreads and deepens. And he extended this juggling with the laws of reality to the laws of painting whose secrets he knew, endowing painting, as the need arose, with new laws.

MASKS CONFRONTING DEATH. 1897

The idea of death consummating the absurdity of life is always present in Ensor. It is rarely macabre; it merely climaxes the strangeness of the universal carnival.

ASTONISHMENT OF THE MASK WOUSE. 1889

SKELETONS TRYING TO WARM THEMSELVES or NO FIRE, WILL YOU GET SOME TOMORROW? 1889

They are ridiculous, these skeleton ghosts shivering in their rags as they crowd about a stove in hopes of regaining some of the warmth of life. However, they provide the painter with a marvelous pretext for the unpredictable play of light and color. Whereas the Late Medieval authors of Dances of Death were inspired by vengeful joy in the idea of universal equality in death, here the stage director is merely brokenhearted. Shall we see in these living dead – one holding a violin, another putting down an unlighted lamp, a third with his palette at his feet – the symbolic representation of the abandoned artist, in search of some encouragement that might bring him back to life, if not today, perhaps tomorrow?

GROTESQUE SINGERS. 1891

Futile whinings, but they proclaim loudly Ensor's caustic spirit, his mastery of, and delight in, painting.

THE ANIMAL MUSICIANS or THE TRAGIC MUSICIANS. 1891

To Ensor, the strange was normal; he worked every conceivable change on it. In "The Animal Musicians" he took pleasure in juxtaposing quite disparate oddities, and intensifying their strangeness by piling them up together — freakish animals, instruments, clothing, glances cast, sounds uttered, as well as freakish fabrics, metals, woods, furs, feathers, scales, and shells, all of which he rendered with consummate skill, proving himself a worthy successor to Bosch and Bruegel.

173

SKELETONS FIGHTING FOR THE BODY OF A HANGED MAN (detail, see c. c. 130). 1891

Futile combats between wretched beings doomed to nothingness. Ensor uses such vaguely infernal scenes to create a paradise of pictorial values.

THE ENTRY OF CHRIST INTO BRUSSELS IN 1889 (detail, see pp. 274, 275). 1888

The large drawing entitled "Hail Jesus, King of the Jews," (p. 150) and perhaps also the 1886 drawing "The Entry of Christ into Jerusalem," may be considered the earliest "versions" of "The Entry of Christ into Brussels." (The etching that bears the same title, which is a fairly accurate reproduction of the canvas, dates from 1898; p. 125). Without being his best work in every respect (the treatment is loose and hasty in some places), this painting is the largest and best known of Ensor's works, and perhaps the most representative. "A work that is gigantic both in its dimensions and in its spirit," says André De Ridder. "A controversial work which will endure, one of the most grandiose artistic creations of our epoch." It may be interesting to recall under what conditions it was painted. Ensor was in straitened circumstances at the time and hesitated to undertake a work that would require a good many tubes of paint. He confided his worries to a house painter who had often expressed his doubts about the quality of paint in the tubes artists used. This workman was kind enough to prepare a number of bright colors in several cans, and Ensor used these rudimentary pigments to cover his canvas. At this time Ensor's studio was a real attic; it had a low ceiling, and there was no wall against which the canvas could be hung at its full height. So Ensor worked on a canvas that was partly nailed to the wall and partly spread on the floor, which obliged him quite often to squat or kneel. When it was completed, the canvas remained rolled up for a long time. Later, after Ensor moved, and the canvas had been framed (this was in 1920), each time it was sent to an exhibition, the iron balcony around the French window in the attic, through which the picture was taken out, had to be loosened. Verhaeren says of this painting that "because of the stinging rawness of the colors, which sometimes suggest poster colors, perhaps also because of the very disorder of the composition, the whole conveys a keen, fierce, and tumultuous sensation of life." To Max Elskamp, Ensor's art "sings in many voices, a strange and sumptuous concert, all plumes, silks, and velvets."

THE DRUNKARDS. 1883

While "Melancholy Fishwives" is almost comical (see p. 187), these drunkards are so much at a loss that they are tragic. It is almost as though Ensor had anticipated the two characters of Samuel Beckett's "Waiting for Godot."

MELANCHOLY FISHWIVES. 1892

Ensor's frequently comical representations of the common people reflect no demands for social justice or other sociological ideas. He sees these men and women as being committed, like everyone else, like himself, to a droll, uncomfortable, incomprehensible, and not infrequently exasperating adventure. While his brush, on occasion, might take the part of the poor against the police, the sobbing, grandiloquent tones used by some of his contemporaries whenever they referred to the common people only aroused his irony. Ensor liked to accompany friends through the fish markets and to provoke the women by jeering at them; they would reply with streams of abuse, and even, now and then, would let fly a fish at him. Far from displeasing him, this delighted and stimulated him.

THE WEIGHT OF THE IMPONDERABLE

Wherever you turn in this unexpected world of Ensor's, you are haunted by a vague disquiet. It is at your back, it nudges you, it whispers in your ear, it sobs, or it sneers in an undertone. This disquiet constitutes the least tangible, but the most important element of Ensor's art, the one element that so many seemingly different canvases have in common.

The solemn peace of his middle-class interiors throbs with nascent fears. In *Haunted Furniture* (c. c. 127) a child has stopped reading to listen to the light footsteps of skeletons rustling by. In the *Grove* (p. 116) and in *Wind* (c. c. 65), the foliage quivers, quickened by invisible presences. Anxiety, if not terror, flashes out of his eyes in Ensor's self-portraits. The *Somber Lady* (p. 57), the *Lady in Distress* (p. 264), and *The Drunkards* (p. 185) feel that the ground on which they stand is giving way. A similar uneasiness pervades the grotesque scenes. The masks look as though the world were foundering. The skeletons' teeth chatter as they make desperate attempts to come back to life. Remote murmurs, indistinct groans, muffled calls for help, sneers, laughs, uncanny cooings are everywhere. When you stop to listen, all is quiet; but these sounds start up again as you turn away. A poetry of anguish communicates and spreads moral disquiet, a poetry that is hard to define, but that is all-pervasive, close to that of Poe, Joyce, or Kafka. It is not so much drama, as an insidious malaise, "nausea," as Sartre would say. The painter seems to be living in a kind of negative universe, to be observing everything from behind the scenes, through peep-holes in the curtain.

Sensitive and emotionally reserved, Ensor was wounded constantly by those around him, by social disappointments, by the poor reception given his works, by life in general. Not being given to complaining, he often relieved himself by jeering, by cultivating in his art the philosophy of the caricaturist. In such moods he was an incorrigible leg-puller, sometimes passionate and sometimes icy, sometimes subtly allusive and sometimes deliberately trivial. This aspect of his art reminds us of his *zwanzes*, charades, and his expeditions with the young Doctor Rousseau who was also a sensitive man who also suffered inwardly from the continual sight of human misery, and who, with Ensor, sought relief in pranks and macabre humor. Sometimes the buffooneries of the artist and the doctor aroused loud laughter in their audience; at other times they merely made everyone uncomfortable. Ensor enjoyed causing embarrassment of this kind, and several of his works bear witness to this tendency. His friend Demolder criticized him for it, writing him from Paris: "Your caricatures are not a bit appreciated. They are regarded as puerile and commonplace." But Ensor did not give up his provoking witticisms, his deliberate and inappropriate rudeness. He let fly in all directions. Stinging as they were, his shafts were often so witty that a good part of their venom disappeared. Ensor the humorist did not try to inflict mortal wounds; he only pretended to murder, the better to kill smugness, conceit, and stupidity. He did not aim at individuals, but at general vices and failings.

This much granted, it must be admitted that he went at it wholeheartedly. Like the good sport he was, he began by making fun of himself, dressing up in silly hats, putting on a ridiculous striped bathing suit, representing himself as pursued by demons or critics, or in the shape of a beetle or a skeleton. Unsparing of himself, he did not spare others. "My favorite occupation," he writes, "is to make others famous, to uglify them, to enrich their ugliness." He assailed his persecutors with vengeful portraits. Like a bull he charged the critics Fétis and Sulzberger who were harassing him with their persistent lack of understanding; he roared at General Leman with whom he had had violent discussions on art at the Rousseaus. He even attacked his own good friends, champions of modern art like Picard, Maus, and others who, true enough, sometimes turned down his works or referred to them with embarrassed evasion. But we must not be misled by all this. His "terrible fits of anger" were less real than simulated; he himself hinted that he was not quite so angry as all that. He proposed a game. Some were unkind enough not to accept its rules.

Playing the critic in his turn, he made fun of himself and made fun of the sentimental art of Jan Van Beers, a fashionable society painter of 1900. In *Beach at Ostend* (p. 123) the target of his sarcasm is a whole beach teeming with bathers and tourists. He enjoyed describing in words the objects of ridicule that the sharp point of his engraving tool picked out: "The beach is extraordinarily animated. It is a strangely mottled world. Swells in well-cut flannels rampant on a field of sand. Mussels heaped upon mussels. Attractive little pieces teasing soft crablike creatures. Slender Englishwomen stride angularly by. Bathers carrying their pachydermic shapes on broad flat feet. Toadlike peasant-women. Screeching females with broad bottoms. Rubes soaping their grimy feet. Grotesque gambolings. A rapacious tribe that sickens all sensitive souls and litters the lovely, delicately toned beach."

Like the anarchistically inclined individualist he was, in *The Bad Doctors* (p. 193), *The Judges* (p. 196), *Gendarmes* (p. 119), and *Belgium in the Nineteenth Century* (p. 152), he attacked the *corps constitués* (officialdom), stigmatizing their shortcomings and stupidities, not always aware how childish his criticisms were in some cases. In *Alimentation Doctrinaire* five men – an officer, a politician, King Leopold II himself, a bishop, and the rector of a university – are shown squatting above the populace, bottoms bared, dropping copious stools upon a waiting crowd with mouths agape, only too happy to receive its nourishment in this fashion. In such pictures, out of cynicism and a taste for the trivial, Ensor, like Bosch and Bruegel, occasionally stooped to the scatological. The stools of King Darius, the jet of urine in *Le Pisseur*, the demons and witches breaking wind, the dung cart in *The Scavenger*, herald the stench – the well-nigh universal stench – of *Peste dessous, peste dessus, peste partout* (c.c. 149).

Why should history, absurdly venerated by painters of an earlier generation, men like Wappers, Slingeneyer, and Gallait, be spared? Breaking with all prevailing attitudes, it is with utter irreverence that Ensor etches the *Battle of Arbela*, the *Roman Triumph* (c. c. 156), *The Battle of the Golden Spurs* (p. 123, c. c. 157), and *Napoleon's Farewell*. Legend is debunked, and reduced to the banal, occasionally comical, dimensions of everyday events. "When I see soldiers parading on formal occasions," he said to Jean Teugels – and his words are characteristic of his attitude to all kinds of decorum, whether military or civilian, whether contemporary or of the past – "my imagination divests them of their decorations, and I see them in their shirt-tails." He is so iconoclastic that he does not shrink from gazing upon the legendary Lady Godiva as she rides naked through Coventry (p. 126, c. c. 167). And what does he see? Two magnificently rounded bottoms, comically superimposed on each other – that of the horse, and that of the heroine who hangs on for dear life.

Over and above such individual, social, and historical comic instances, Ensor perceived a vaster, more universal comedy. To express it, he made use of bizarre juxtapositions of elements drawn from disparate portions of nature – not unlike the practice of Schongauer, Bosch, Callot, and Grandville before him. He "humanizes" insects, "animalizes" people, and manufactures monsters by combining heterogeneous elements that happen to be at hand or that pop into his mind. *Odd Insects* (p. 118), *Devils' Sabbath* (p. 122), *Combat of Demons* (p. 122), *Bizarre Little Figures*, and *The Tragic Musicians* (p. 173) portray nature as an enormous alchemist's crucible, out of which steps a mad parade of fantastic biological forms.

Apollinaire wrote to Severini: "You will realize later that the spirit of caricature has played an important part in the development of modern art." There is no clear demarcation between caricature and expression, and it is not surprising that artists bent on achieving the utmost in expression, such as Daumier, Toulouse-Lautrec, Ensor, and Picasso (and we might go back as far as Bruegel and Leonardo) should have come close to caricature or even practiced it consciously.

SKELETONS DISPUTING A HERRING. 1891

The wordplay in the French title ("hareng saur/art Ensor") suggests that this dazzling piece of painting represents two critics brutally attacking Ensor's art.

THE BAD DOCTORS. 1895

Sometimes Ensor retouched an etching, turning it into a little painting flooded with delicate light and rich in subtle colors.

193

light, its planes, its gravitations. These progressive explorations modify the original vision, and the line suffers and is relegated to a secondary role. This vision will be little comprehended. It requires long observation and attentive study. The vulgar herd sees in it only disorder, chaos, and inaccuracy." Remarks of this kind are scattered throughout Ensor's writings. They are strikingly true, and illuminate a number of artistic problems which only artists can feel and express so aptly.

He wrote one sentence that has become famous, the vigorous and ferocious maxim which he took as his own motto: *Les suffisances matamoresques appellent la finale crevaison grenouillère* (freely: "The frog that croaks the loudest is closest to bursting").

THE JUDGES. 1891

Ensor, who was anarchistically inclined, liked to make sarcastic observations at the expense of all official bodies. Although he did not shrink from crude irony, he never failed to translate it into color.

ANGUISH AND IRONY

The alliance between gravity and buffoonery is one of the most original features of Ensor's mind. His laughter, whether open or secret, at some of the least funny spectacles of life may seem out of place, but it was natural to him.

Not that he was insensitive. The dramas of life touched his mind and heart. He had intimate knowledge of shattered hopes, of disgust and terror, and he was a pitiless observer of moral wretchedness, social abuses, inner conflicts, frustrated ambitions; he was ever conscious of death, the ineluctable end of human strivings. But where others lament, he ironized, out of pride, out of a sense of dignity. Like Vigny, like Montherlant, he indulged in the spiritual luxury of despising fate. More aware and more vulnerable than others, he behaved *as if* the sinister human adventure were but a game, and did not touch him. "There is a kind of laughter," says Gogol, who was an expert in irony, "that ranks with the loftiest lyrical emotions, and that is at an astronomical distance from vulgar clowning." Ensor's laughter is very much of this kind. He puts happy masks on the saddest faces, and dresses his corpses in holiday finery instead of shrouds.

Joy, in Ensor, takes multiple forms. Traditional psychology would be hard put to it to classify them: they are an artist's joys, they are expressed wholly in painters' terms, and have no recourse to symbolic representations of joy. Likewise, there is a musician's humor, that of a Satie, for example, and a poet's humor, that of a Rimbaud, a Lautréamont, a Raymond Queneau. The pleasure comes less from the subject treated than from the manner of treating it, from the treatment itself. Ensor's laughter is inseparable from his technique – grim or gay, bright vermilion or electric blue, sly half-smiles in the shadows, recurrent "yellow" (sickly) laughter, laughter in dotted lines, in flat tints, in delicately graduated washes – his laughter is as varied as the innumerable mixtures that can be made from the colors of his palette.

It is said that Frans Hals renders masterfully the play of muscles and the other indications of joy on the human face: his works could serve as illustrations for a book on the psychology of laughter. Ensor, however, does not try to paint laughing faces. In drawing faces and in choosing his colors he was guided by a perpetually present inner amusement. To the colors on his palette corresponds a gamut of types of laughter. But he would deliberately slip in a note of the macabre, to jolt those who laugh too easily.

But ultimately, one may ask, is there a sense of the tragic in Ensor? The answer to this question is "No," if we think that everything was for him an amusing game. It is "Yes," if we consider that the game he proposed was sinister of itself, or if we suspect that it frightened him. According to certain psychologists, a child can be mortally frightened by the roar of a lion he nevertheless knows not to be "real."

MAN OF SORROWS. 1891

Ensor here discloses a deeply hidden aspect of his thought and his art. In the colors of blood and anger, transmuted by his artistic will, in the petals of roses and mignonettes, there is withal a grimace of pain and impotent rage, which puts furrows in the brow, makes the nostrils quiver, and twists the mouth. Divested of its mask at last, a face reveals an unbearable contortion of the whole being before the inanity of life.

AFFINITY FOR CHRIST

How frequently Christ occurs in the work of this allegedly anti-religious painter! Christ adored by the Magi and the shepherds, Christ in the temple, Christ tempted by devils, Christ calming the waters, Christ received in triumph, Christ insulted, Christ flogged, Christ stumbling under the burden of the Cross, Christ crucified, Christ resurrected, Christ descended into Hell. A whole cycle of the life of Christ, episode by episode.

Ensor's Christ is a lonely figure, lost in the crowd, glowing with a hidden light. Only rarely does His light burst forth in a cosmic radiance. While everything in Ensor is chaos, there nonetheless appears in his absurd universe – as a sort of complement to the absurdity – a glimpse of some paradisiac oasis, a garden of love filled with rosy blond nymphs, a Christ impervious to evil, as absurd in His incorruptibility as the dull, grotesque tribe that absurdly ignores, hails, and persecutes Him.

Ensor liked to read the New Testament, to rediscover human folly in it, and to sympathize with its hero. He rejected traditional Christianity: this is understandable in the light of his upbringing, his personality, and his friendships with nonbelievers. At the same time, Jesus seemed to him as a person free and courageous, attractive both in His anarchism and His serenity, and he celebrated Him with all his verve, not in a mystic spirit, but in a lyrical one, and always with reverence. Clearly, Christ was to Ensor what He was to Bosch, a luminous presence swallowed up in the legions of the mad.

With his pointed beard and his long hair, Ensor physically resembled the traditional image of Christ. Because, too, he felt himself misunderstood and maltreated as a man and as an artist, he needed no more than this resemblance to represent himself as Christ, exposed to mockery, nailed to the Cross by his critics. This time, Ensor, who loved all games, indulged in the game of identification. But let there be no mistake about it: the fact that he sometimes identified himself with God did not prevent Ensor, always ambivalent, to identify himself occasionally with the Devil.

ECCE HOMO or CHRIST AND HIS CRITICS. 1891

At the center we see Ensor crowned with thorns, a rope around his neck, receiving the derisory scepter from one of his persecutors. He is flanked by two of his most aggressive critics, Max Sulzberger (at the right) and Edouard Fétis (at the left). "Fétis tore at me with his brittle old fingernails," we read in Ensor's "Ecrits." This delightful little cartoon is characterized by unusual keenness in the drawing and great subtlety of color.

CONSOLING VIRGIN. 1892

This work, a personal confession dating from his best period, is conceived as an Annunciation in which the Virgin plays the part of the angel and the artist that of the Virgin. Ensor represented himself as he always was, in love with painting, kneeling humbly before and ready to receive the blessing of celestial intervention. He expressed his veneration in the Symbolist fashion, in the manner of a Burne-Jones or a Khnopff, but he also gave the painting some of the simplicity and fervor of the Italian primitives.

The world seems attractive to Ensor by virtue of its prodigious vitality; what disillusions him is the way everything is subjected to the crushing law of death. Its vitality, he first of all found in himself, an ultra-sensitive receiving apparatus, a passionate spectator within whom teemed a marvelous world of sensations, impulses, and ever-renewed thoughts. Thus, to him, the self became the very image of life. "I want to recount to everyone the lovely legend of the self," he proclaimed, "of the universal self, the unique self, the big-bellied self, the great verb TO BE." In the face of this SELF, doubtless to bring it into greater relief, he set the "anti-self," death symbolized by the skeleton.

We encounter Ensor's "self," receiving apparatus of life, center of being and of consciousness, everywhere in his art. Ensor with his palette, Ensor at the easel, Ensor writing, Ensor at the piano, Ensor drawing, Ensor in a flowered hat, Ensor with masks, Ensor as a fighting cock, Ensor in a bathing suit, Ensor as an insect, Ensor kneeling, Ensor beheaded, Ensor the target of scurrilous jokes, Ensor crowned with thorns, Ensor under investigation, Ensor on the Cross, Ensor in Hell. But all around him, everywhere in his works, the skeleton appears also – skeletons in his studio, skeletons trying to warm themselves, a skeleton examining Chinese curios, a skeleton pursuing the human herd, skeletons seated in easy chairs, hidden behind pieces of furniture, skeletons at the Carnival, in the woods, on the beach, in the sky. All these skeletons are alive and active because, as Ensor sees it, death is not a vague future; death is a continuous presence, dwelling in the very midst of life.

Finally, diverted by the game, Ensor brings together the "self," symbol of life, with the skeleton, symbol of death. Thus he comes to "skeletonize" his own portrait (c. c. 25). It is in the spirit that he executed the little etching representing a collapsed skeleton bathed in a soft light, soon to be no more than a little pile of ashes, an etching which he entitled *My Portrait in 1960* (p. 206). Marked by a sense of mockery, an unemphatic expression of the struggle between the self and annihilation – a struggle lost in advance – this minuscule work is the epitome of Ensor's art. In it we find the duality of feeling so characteristic of Ensor, setting drama and irony against each other to their mutual disparagement.

This self of Ensor's, at once rebellious and yet constrained by the inevitable, spiteful, dignified, proud, and genuinely amused at the enormity of its defeat, chooses to laugh in the teeth of a pitiless fate.

THE SMELL OF DEATH AND THE FRAGRANCE OF THE FEAST

Grégoire Le Roy asks whether anyone else has noted "the unbreathable air, the strange atmosphere, the unreal space in those scenes of skeletons and masks, dressed up in improbable garb?" Here the living who are doomed to die come into contact with and breathe an air from beyond the grave, an air the dead bring with them when, to re-enter the land of the living, they become ghosts.

Even in his "somber" period, it would seem that Ensor had glimpsed under the murky colors he used at the time, the rustling sounds made by the comings and goings of faintly groaning presences. Soon they were to emerge out of invisibility and to adhere to walls, to creep over rugs. Ensor had glimpses of them as they surrounded women while they sewed or took naps, and children as they dreamed. Dream and reality, like life and death, become indistinguishable. And finally there is a whole repertory of specters, absent-minded, enjoying themselves, harassing and teasing an anxious mankind ill-at-ease and uncertain as to what to make of them. Everything takes on the taste of ashes, the color of faded leaves and wilted flowers, the weary inflections of dying forms. "Macabre dances" are organized. The wind of panic blows through hysterical groups of stampeding revelers; routed, the crowd surges wildly forward into the gates of nothingness. The last mask, the face of flesh that covered the face of bones, is pitilessly ripped off.

Ensor faced misfortune bravely. Asked what death he would prefer, he answered, "That of a flea crushed on a virgin's white breast." This is the answer certain of his works make to others. Weary of horror, they occasionally – rarely, save in the last years – become warm and charming. To the sound of mandolins, princes and princesses, elves and fairies exchange graceful greetings. Ballerinas in tutus skip over a ground strewn with flowers. Preparing for the fete in costumes of silk, Columbines and Harlequins step lightly through Gardens of Love. There were even some delightful erotic miniatures, but they were destroyed by sacrilegious hands. However, if you look carefully, you will glimpse, amidst these unexpected moments of euphoria, here and there, a devil's cloven hoof peeping out from a velvet cloak, or a devil's horns under a feathered hat.

My Portrait in 1960. 1880

Slowly, very slowly the wall of incomprehension surrounding the undesirable *ving-tiste* began to crumble. Ensor himself took note of it: "A reaction is beginning to take shape, enthusiasts are beginning to praise the exceptional painter, the occasional composer, the poet without rhyme or reason." Publication, in 1899, of an issue of *La Plume* devoted entirely to Ensor, set the ball rolling. It was his friend Eugène Demolder – "Fridolin" had baptized him "Gragapança d'Yppredamme" – who used his influence with his Paris friends to bring out the issue (*La Plume* being an *avant-garde* French publication). Despite the undeniable interest of this issue, and despite the fact that Lemmonier, Verhaeren, Maeterlinck, Elskamp, Demolder, and Blanche Rousseau all contributed to it, it passed almost entirely unnoticed. Neither sponsor nor artist was satisfied; the former accused his friend of having chosen too many works with a caricatural emphasis; the latter felt that some of the essays, particularly one by Delattre, "teemed with exaggerations and inaccuracies."

Here and there, however, individuals began to be intrigued by the singularity and the rare technical qualities of the Ostend "madman's" works, His name appeared in Italian, German, and Dutch publications. But not until 1908 did a substantial study, by the poet Verhaeren, appear; it was then that Ensor recalled just how long he had had to wait. "At first almost totally alone, I waited for a long time. Later came lively excitement. Verhaeren made great sweeping gestures in the direction of imaginary horizons; Demolder wrote in tribute to the truculent painter, drinking to his health; Des Ombiaux, the bantering connoisseur, comforted us; Giraud gave lectures; Mockel sighed; Maus smiled, Lemonnier roared .... Verlaine honored me with an absinth hiccup. Van de Woestijne, who looks like an archbishop, flung his ruby-studded staff into the fray ...."

In 1896 the Brussels museum went so far as to purchase Ensor's least compromising canvas, *The Lamp Boy* (p. 33). Until this time the Rousseaus had been almost his only collectors. They certainly liked what they bought, but they also bought out of friendship and to encourage him, to get him "started." Not very often, and always at modest prices, one or another of his less aggressive works found a buyer. A real wave of buying began in 1900, and gathered strength shortly after the first World War. During and after the second World War, dealers and collectors alike became increasingly eager, and all but indecent in their insistence.

Portrait of Emil Verhaeren. 1890

UNEXPECTED COLLAPSE

What happened? Toward 1900, when the hostility against him began slowly to yield to admiration, Ensor, who had almost reached the mid-point of his life, who was in the prime of life, seemed to falter. While he did not give up painting, and continued to draw and to write, he was no longer the magnificent inventor, as individualistic, as fertile, as daring as he had been. Something in him had snapped. The essential, imperious, fierce creative energy that had dwelled in him was gone. Among a number of almost insignificant works, he was still to produce some very fine ones, but the continuous stream of ever-new creations had run dry.

What caused this untoward downfall? Was he stricken with some nervous or circulatory disease? Nothing in the published record, nor in his correspondence justifies such an assertion. Was he the victim of one of those "regressions" so dear to the psychoanalysts, which make the adult go back to the timidities of pre-adolescence, and of which Racine is supposed to be one of the most famous examples? As in the case of Gezelle or Rimbaud, the crisis was no doubt moral rather than physical. Such a hypothesis is supported by Ensor's circumstances at the time. The critics, the public, those closest to him, his fellow artists of Les XX, the holders of official power (those he called *les bourreaux de bureaux* – "the executive executioners") had all dealt harshly with him, and he had been wounded deeply. He had come to doubt himself, had fits of depression, and, as his intimates relate, had wept with despair. His powers of resistance had been broken. And he had less power of resistance than appeared on the surface. While as an artist he was able to take refuge in his studio, and there to be combative and full of spunk, as a man at grips with the "outside world," he was hesitant, weak, and very vulnerable. After so many years of struggle, he took praise skeptically, and often accepted it with a bitter smile. He doubted his admirers' sincerity and truthfulness, and he expected more malicious attacks and fresh misunderstanding at any moment.

La Sirène (Mlle. Boogaerts). c. 1920

The Rousseaus' home in Brussels had lost its stimulating and irreverent atmosphere. Professor Rousseau, who had held the circle of friends together, was now old, and for reasons of health, spent his winters in Nice. His son lost his young wife and remained inconsolable; moreover, as a result of his work with the microscope, he was afflicted with a temporary blindness. The former liveliness that had marked the gatherings in the Rue Vautier was gone; the spell was broken. Ensor was deprived of a much-needed source of encouragement. He went to Brussels more and more rarely, and kept up only from a distance with his friends who were now scattered. He had no choice but to fall back on the resources of Ostend. Here he was bitterly reproached for doing only what amused him and never trying to earn money. His mother harped constantly on this subject, and his aunt and sister echoed her. In the eyes of his family, his work was valueless, his painting silly and useless. His father, the only person close to him who had warmer feelings, who was interested in music and was pleased to see him painting, had died. James, who loathed travel and disliked all change, decided to go to London, to his father's mother, hoping that she would give him some comfort. He found a venerable old lady who received him politely but coldly; she had not forgotten that her son had married beneath his station. Disgusted, James returned to the tired and sullen women in Ostend, whom he used as models for the drawing *Sloth* (p. 64), and who actually spent the eight months of the off season in a state resembling hibernation.

He had to admit that the financial returns from his art were ridiculous. He tried hard to sell *Afternoon at Ostend* (pp. 53, 55), a canvas he loved, but it always came back, rejected; although he set a modest price on it, he never sold it. Out of spite he took the canvas out of its frame, and used it as a studio rug for the edification of his friends. On another occasion, in a fit of despair, he tried to sell all his works, everything in his studio, for a mere 8,000 francs. This, too, failed, despite the repeated, almost embarrassingly determined efforts of his friends to find buyers.

In the meantime, while his major works, those into which he had put the best of himself, were ignored, his growing reputation induced one or another amateur to commission him to paint one of his "drolleries," a little as one asks a clown to be funny. On such occasions, the family was impressed and encouraged him.

Augusta Boogaerts, daughter of an Ostend hotel owner, who had been a salesgirl in the Ensors' souvenir shop, visited him regularly. Augusta whom he called "La Sirène" was never actually to live with him, but remained his lifelong *amie*. Caustic, an alert observer, with an enigmatic smile forever on her lips, she was capable of unexpectedly sharp repartee, which made her attractive, but also a bit awesome. An undeclared war between her and the painter's family was to continue indefinitely.

"La Sirène" wanted to marry him; his relatives opposed this idea with all their strength, and won. Sordid money questions aggravated the disputes. This did not do anything to improve the atmosphere of the household.

Ensor defended himself as best he could, dodging issues, withdrawing into himself, proud, sarcastic, evasive, and impenetrable. He took petty revenge on "the weaker sex" by apostrophizing it as follows: "Deceiving sex, respector neither of law nor of religion, sink of hypocrisy, bastion of malice, beast with claws and suckers, and teeth for tearing live flesh, feather-brained goose, creaky weather vane responsive to every ill wind, constant mask and endless smile . . . ."

He amused himself as best he could, but at bottom he was helpless. He could no longer play, or laugh, or jeer. He tried to paint again, but halfheartedly; the sacred fire had gone out. To his surprise, he was no longer scolded, but on the contrary, urged to work. His games were no longer played earnestly, he merely tried to give the impression that he was playing. From this time onward, his "moral temperature," in Taine's phrase, remained below the level essential to genius.

This misfortune is primarily accounted for by the fact that Ensor the lover of games, Ensor the dreamer and scoffer, had been brought down to the everyday level of life. His delight in play, faced with the contempt of those who did not accept the rules of his game, had vanished. Like those other "madmen" – Lautréamont, Laforgue, Van Gogh, Rimbaud, the less well known, and all those unknowns who have left no traces – Ensor was defeated by the down-to-earth, "practical" middle-class spirit, by what Mallarmé called "The disheartening necessity of expending one's angelic faculties in defense of one's own privacy, against the pushing, shoving assaults of the everyday enemy: people."

It is also possible that Ensor did not have much more to add to what he had already said. Perhaps it was in the very nature of his art, spasmodic manifestation of a mind touched to the quick, that it never became one continuous, uninterrupted song, essentially peaceful like Corot's or essentially joyful like Renoir's.

THE LAST PERIOD

Ensor's last period was the least inventive one, but by far the longest. Whereas the "somber" period lasted barely five years and the "light" period about fifteen, the last period, which might be called the "crystalline," extended over approximately fifty years. It is characterized by fluid colors that scarcely cover the canvas, by tones simultaneously vivid and blurry, a hesitant, not to say wavering, line, and the absence of internal structure. The best works of this period have a freedom of color and a luminosity that bring them close to Fauvism, of which Ensor, by virtue of his over-all contribution, is a brilliant precursor. The least good ones are painfully elaborate and puerile. Alongside a few canvases of very high quality, such as the Strindbergian *Double Portrait* (The Artist and Mlle. Auguste Boogaerts) (p. 347) which stands out remarkably from the rest, *Deliverance of Andromeda* (c. c. 166), *Moses and the Birds* (c. c. 165), *Port of Ostend* (p. 223), *Ensor at the Harmonium* (p. 217), *Vengeance of Hop Frog* (p. 225), and particularly *Afternoon at Ostend* (light version; p. 222), there are dozens unworthy of their author, lacking the presence of that imponderable something, which was the best part of Ensor's previous work.

Just as each work before 1900 reflects an original idea, a strong and unique perception, so the works after 1900 are completely lacking in invention, and in most cases reflect a pre-established technical system and intellectual attitude. Ensor, who until 1900 had repeated himself less than anyone else, was now to repeat himself more than anyone else. He no longer sought his themes in nature, in his imagination, or in the possible variations of a continually renewed technique, but almost exclusively in his previous works. He systematically plagiarized himself. He redid the old pictures several times, and the successive versions become less and less good; he recomposed in brilliant colors a number of works of his "somber" period (and occasionally these replicas are of a marvelous coloristic subtlety). He painted from old sketches and old engravings; he went so far as to make tracings of his old drawings. Worse than that:

knowing that his earlier works were valued more highly, he back-dated paintings and drawings. None of this helped his reputation; his reproduction of major works in a minor key casts discredit on his art as a whole.

A similar decline of vigor is discernible in his writing. Although the form still strives for maliciousness, the substance tends to be complacent. According to Grégoire Le Roy, "Ensor now keeps the button on his rapier. His satire is smothered under flowery decoration." Jules Renard was similarly conscious of a falling-off: "Our nastiness carried to that point," he writes, "loses all significance. It is no more than mental gymnastics. We are nasty for the fun of it, idly amusing ourselves with a toy that is difficult to handle, but we no longer want to hurt anyone." And Pierre Schneider, Jules Renard's biographer, adds: "The bourgeois are the first to be amused by the pretended ferocity of the attacks against them, against the established order, and against the police." The aged Ensor knew this, and acknowledged, not without bitterness, that he had become "a harmless entertainer."

Program of the Game of Love, with an autograph dedication by Ensor

ESCAPE INTO MUSIC

When Ensor was told that his painting was admired and his writings read with delight, he would answer that he had taken the wrong path and that he should have devoted himself entirely to music. Then he would sit down at the piano or the harmonium and improvise, producing a graceful succession of crystalline and high-pitched notes, cascading pearls, swirling confetti. There is no way of saying what he might have composed during his great years: the musical works he actually produced are the equivalent of his sugar-coated canvases and mellower writings. We have only one sample of the music he produced in his decline, the ballet *La Gamme d'Amour* (The Game of Love) composed in 1911 – as weak musically as his scenic designs, dating from the same period, for the ballet, are pictorially weak (c. c. 179, 180). The sputtering and anodyne music for *La Gamme d'Amour* is far from achieving the quality of the triumphant and jarring music suggested by Ensor in 1891, when he painted *Music, Rue de Flandre* (p. 49), and *The Tragic Musicians* (p. 173).

We know that, although he amused himself in his youth by playing the flute through his nose and playing the piano while sitting with his back to the keyboard, he would frequently, when he was irritated by the people around him, suddenly break his silence and let off steam at the piano, improvising a music so bizarre and violent that the company would be struck dumb.

He had never studied music, but in this field, too, he was one of those who know without learning: music lived within him. Sensitive as he was to analogies between sensations, to correspondences between the arts, we must grant, as he himself said, that he often painted as a musician, and that his canvases are full of musical elements.

ENSOR AT THE HARMONIUM. 1933

The artist is seen here as he had really become in his old age, the curator of his own works, always ready to play for visitors one of the droll musical compositions which never failed to baffle them. This work is characteristic of Ensor's last manner, at once sweet and sharp, soft and brittle, with the color wavering between the thin and the saturated. This final tendency of Ensor's is not unlike that of the last Renoirs and the last Utrillos.

216

Ensor's coat-of-arms

SLOW RISE TO FAME

While Ensor, at a complete loss, made desperate efforts to reconquer his talent, tributes to his art piled up around him. Respected by artists at home and abroad, he was also showered with official honors. During the last fifty years of his life and uninterruptedly thereafter, his fame steadily grew and the chorus of praise became increasingly louder. His work was discussed in publication after publication, awards and honors poured in from everywhere, collectors and dealers pampered him, *avant-garde* groups elected him honorary member, he was begged to take part in exhibitions, museums fought for his canvases, and great art societies, the Belgian government as well as foreign countries, organized retrospective shows of his works. He was made a Baron by the king, and besides banquets in his honor, he attended the unveiling of a monument to himself.

In 1917 an uncle left him the house next door to the one in which he had produced his masterpieces. Like all the family houses it included a souvenir shop on the ground floor. Ensor moved into that house. He kept the shop (although he did not run it), and made his living quarters on the second floor, using the floor above that as his studio, where he hung a number of his best canvases, among them the enormous *Entry of Christ into Brussels* (pp. 181, 274, 275). What he had created in the attic studio of the house next door he now exhibited in his drawing-room studio. This drawing room became famous. It was a fairyland of colors, an enchantment to the eye. One entered it with a feeling of veneration. Many distinguished guests, including princes of finance, of art, of science, and of politics, made their way into it.

The man who only yesterday had been "undesirable" became a national figure. He had traded his young man's face – that of a laughing, insolent devil, set off by jet-black curls – for the face of a handsome old man with full lips, eyes as blue as the deepest seas, and wavy white hair and beard, of a white that sparkled with brilliant beige and bluish highlights. Tall, always dressed in black, with a flowing tie and an ample cape over his shoulders, he was most impressive to look at. Physically he belonged to the same type as those other grand old men – Anatole France, Claude Monet, Aristide Maillol, and Bernard Shaw. Hospitable, amiable, witty, he nevertheless remained impenetrable. He would burst out laughing at any moment: he laughed at himself with bitterness but without rancor, and at others without malice. Readily obliging his visitors, he would improvise on the piano or the harmonium. He would give an advance reading of his latest prose, pieces in which he took digs at people but without clawing them, as irreverent as his visitors asked him to be, almost politely so.

Would he have gone on painting if those around him had not urged him to do so? His canvases and panels were prepared for him; his old drawings were rummaged through for models of suitably "Ensorian" subjects. "La Sirène" was particularly diligent. She would arrange still-life compositions of shells, masks, dried flowers, and Chinese trinkets, and lead James, palette in hand, to his subject. During Ensor's last years she played the role that Lucie Valore was shortly to play for the aged, tired Utrillo. She would supervise his production, keeping a careful inventory of it, and promoted sales, making the decisions regarding printing the engravings. Ensor did not always give in to her, and we witness petty fights like this one: One day Ensor expected "La Sirène" to come by the studio, but he had to go out. He left a note for her: "Do not take anything; I have counted everything." On his return he found another note, saying: "Don't count anything; I have taken everything."

The atmosphere surrounding the now famous master was almost Balzacian. Ensor would probably have preferred to execute harmless plates of the type of *The Seven Deadly Sins* (pp. 158, 159; c. c. 152, 153) rather than to see them circle around him in flesh and blood and "bother" him. But he was now armored with a blessed and solid indifference. He had become to others and perhaps also to himself a *stranger*, wearing the mask of an artist in cape and flowing tie, but himself absent, inaccessible. Occasionally however, he could be scathing in speaking of himself: "Here is the old man gone gray in harness, bent under the yoke of exaggerated tributes." Referring to his ennoblement, he spoke of "that poor bovine baron who will soon be chewing the cud of choice infusions and the bitter sap of faded laurels." In 1935, when he painted a fairly mediocre self-portrait after so many others that are masterpieces, he wrote on the canvas: "This portrait, like its author, is about ready to cave in." His only pleasure now was to hurt himself.

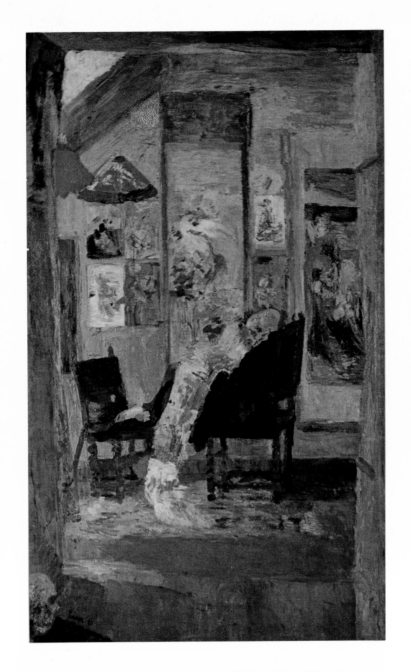

SKELETON LOOKING AT CHINOISERIES. 1885

Admiration for the Far East, such as was expressed by certain Impressionists and by the Nabis, was also shared by Ensor. The Oriental trinkets he found in his parents' shop inspired him. In this image of death engrossed in the contemplation of pretty Oriental objects, the idea of escape into refinement may be implied, an idea which is reinforced by the technical refinements in the painting itself.

AFTERNOON AT OSTEND (light version). About 1910

Almost all the replicas that Ensor made of his own paintings are literal copies, inferior to the originals. But occasionally the new work is a true re-creation. Such is the case with this "light" version of "Afternoon at Ostend." The subdued misty tones of the first version (see p. 53) have been banished and replaced by a clear golden light. The light, rapid brushwork has covered the canvas with iridescent and translucent tones. The forms remain intangible, but instead of being submerged in shadow, they are dissolved in light.

PORT OF OSTEND, TWILIGHT IN STORMY WEATHER. 1933

This work is characteristic of Ensor's last manner. Not without charm and refinement, it shows traces of weariness, the color having lost its emphasis, and the drawing its vigor. But it remains an attractive work, with an unexpected range of tones, delicacy of lighting, and a suggestion of Ensor's former strangeness.

THE VENGEANCE OF HOP FROG (after the tale by Edgar Allan Poe). Back-dated 1896, probably painted about 1910

Ensor had profound affinities with Edgar Allan Poe, the poet who said he was tormented by the Angel of the Bizarre. This painting was done from the etching of the same subject, which Ensor had made in 1898. Whereas the engraving reveals an exceptional visionary gift and a marvelous inventive power, the painting lacks the vividness and the sharp expressiveness of each detail in the print (see p. 128). But the painted version has a rare brilliance of color which makes it more than a mere replica.

With all his energetic capacity for admiring life, with all his avidity for seizing multiplicity, for idling, for inventing, for improvising – and his taste for such things was unlimited in the period of his full creative vigor – Ensor turned against rationalism and disputed the validity of classicism. He was determined to be free to paint what he pleased and as he pleased. "Reason is the enemy of art," he exclaimed. "Artists dominated by reason lose all feeling, their powerful instinct weakens, their inspiration is impoverished, their heart loses its vital spirit . . . . All rules, all canons of art belch death." He rejected all systems of measurements, all recourse to "the golden section," all the encroachments of science on art. He resented the labels invented by critics: "O the villains who catalogue artists! If these launchers of May flies had their way, adorable fantasy, the heavenly flower of dew which inspires the creative artist would be rigorously excluded from the program of art." He repudiated the doctrinaire: "The boiled potatoes some people throw at one, should be preferred to the apples picked from the old tree of science." He even attacks the pillars of the temple of rationalism: "Above all else let us condemn the infamous doctrines of Descartes, that platitudinous valet to the odious Christina of Sweden, and the stupid Malebranche; the doctrines of these unwholesome men tend to sterilize the heart in the name of reason."

Endowed with a versatile mind, he was an Impressionist in the moral and literary sense of the term rather than by virtue of his pictorial technique. Continually captivated by new sensations, by new spiritual positions, he never stopped adapting his mode of expression to the pirouettes of his unstable self. He was an extreme individualist, one not content simply to cultivate personal views in sharp contrast with most of the people around him, but one who stopped at each of his provisional stages. He did not merely "individualize" himself, he "momentarized" himself. As he did so, he disintegrated, risking dissolution in the sea of pluralities, but at the same time multiplying himself and becoming more universal – in a quite different sense from the humanists, who centralize and syncretize. Fanatic on the score of the multiplicity of the self, he rebelled instinctively against all efforts to level and regiment the individual. The collectivity frightened him; even public tribute seemed to him an entering wedge for suppression. "Why satisfy the vile desire of the crowd," he said, "a desire without nobility, a curiosity that weighs heavily upon us, the supersensitive. Let us resist communion with the mob! To be artists, let us live in hiding!"

His position is clear: he was partisan of total gratuitousness, of instability, of unreason, of perpetual renewal. He was on Beelzebub's side against Apollo, for the Nordics and against the Greeks and Romans, for Shakespeare and against Corneille, for Grünewald and against Raphael. Today he would accept Chagall and reject Lhote and Léger; no doubt he would hail the Surrealists and turn his back on the "abstract" artists. In saying this, I may be going too far, because his taste for variety inclined him to permit everything save that which sets itself up as exclusively valid. In brief, his only rule of conduct was not to follow any rules, whether in drawing, in orchestrating color, in the choice of subjects, or in composition. He wanted to keep himself open to influence, to adapt at will, to dream, to indulge in whims, to be as unpredictable to himself as to others. Too much in love with everything to become attached to anything, too ardent not to go to extremes each time, he welcomed variations and contradictions, was friend alike to God and the Devil, delighted in sweetness and in tragedy, was equally intoxicated with life and with death. Basically agnostic, he relied on chance. Hence the capriciousness of his compositions, his abrupt *volte-faces*, his colors and characters that drift along, his actions without rhyme or reason, his moments of pure bizarrerie. Hence also his vision of the world as a comedy, a game, a masquerade, and the little importance he attached to his own fate, to the vain agitations and strivings of mankind, to the caprice of passion, and to the arbitrariness of death.

Such tidal waves of absurdity nourished his skepticism, and he devoted himself joyously to painting. Ensor would have agreed with Schopenhauer's saying, "Art is the only remedy against the malady of existence." But Ensor who was less pessimistic, and who possessed great talent, might more aptly have said: "Art, the ultimate pleasure amidst the accidents of existence." And did he not write this, so characteristic of his lifelong attitude: "Even when I had the blues, I saw everything through rose-colored glasses." And this, too: "The welling-up of our joy, quickened by grief, promises us a paradise peopled with delights." But we should perhaps remember Ensor as he once painted himself, kneeling before the *Consoling Virgin* (p. 203), personification of the goddess Painting, of whom he once said: "I had a glimpse of the Consoling Virgin, and I recorded her graceful features on a panel of good quality. I was quite young then. I felt the material of her blond cloak, I kissed her little feet of snow and mother-of-pearl. On the hard substance of the old panel the diaphanous image can still be made out; I guard it jealously; it is mine, and I love it." His exclusive, almost morbid love for painting determined Ensor's character and made him the baffling man he was. The beauty, the comedy, and the seamy side of life, in all their extremes, stirred not Ensor the man, but Ensor the painter and artist. To him, painting was a kind of thick glass wall, which, though translucent and light-giving, cut him off from ordinary living. This great adventurer, this daredevil – one of the most daring in the history of painting – was the most timorous of men in everyday circumstances. He turned his back on the common lot of mankind the better to convey his message to us. It may be asked whether he experienced love, joy, hatred, despair, fear, or enthusiasm otherwise than as he projected them in his painting. But was this not the price he paid for his extreme sensitivity, and must we not say of him what Suzanne Lilar says of poets – that in order to reconcile themselves to passion and terror, they must integrate them into a system of forms which makes them bearable?

But can art continue to feed on its own resources, without drawing upon an ardently lived non-artistic life around it? Possibly Ensor's consistent aloofness from life, which had become a habit, almost a vice, ended by undermining his talent, and accounts in part for the weakness of his later works. Can we hold this against him? The efforts to silence him during his magnificently carefree years were cruel; it would be cruel now to reproach him for having given in. The responsibility for what might

THE CUIRASSIERS AT WATERLOO or NAPOLEON'S LAST STAND. 1891

Ensor is skillful at depicting crowds in motion. He endows them with an epic quality without being obvious, and by the means and magic of his art gives their movements a cosmic connotation.

be called his "abdication" devolves upon those to whom he tried to "offer" his works but who, as he said sadly, "did not care for them at all."

It would be erroneous and unfair to accuse him of cowardice. A great deal of courage had been required at the beginning of his career to turn his back on everyday reality so as to produce his most vigorous works; and he cut himself off so completely that he was incapable, at the end of his career, of resisting the degradation of his art. To condemn him would be like condemning the doctor who has become crippled as a result of heroic experiments upon himself, or the soldier who is wounded on the battlefield. Ensor was a less spectacular kind of hero. To be sure, we may deplore the fact that his heroism led him in the end into absurdity; but we must not forget that it had enabled the young Ensor to give us an impressive series of masterpieces, a new method of perceiving and interpreting the world, and of using pictorial language – in short, an original, highly personal aesthetic system.

A ROYAL FUNERAL

Ensor's fame kept on growing, and he was nearly ninety when he died at Ostend. He was given a king's funeral. The whole city, the whole of Belgium accompanied him to the grave. The last procession through the streets of Ostend could not fail to evoke the carnival-like *Entry of Christ into Brussels* (pp. 181, 274, 275), which he had painted more than a half century earlier. Around the sacred relic – in the picture it had been the small, haloed figure of the god on a donkey, but now it was the painter's own coffin – swirled just such an absurd tide of humanity as Ensor had painted in his heyday. Among the swarming mass were Cabinet ministers in full regalia, ambassadors in their cocked hats, church dignitaries in red and lace, mustachioed generals in showy uniforms, critics sharpening their pens, severely frowning magistrates, schoolboys lined up in rows, the fishermen of Ostend in their traditional brown, the gaping curious, fishwives aroused from their melancholia. Brass bands played, church bells rang out, orators delivered high-sounding eulogies, flags flew at half-mast. All that was lacking to make the masquerade complete were delegations of animal musicians and grimacing fishes, summer vacationists in their bathing suits, hilarious devils, fairies in mourning, and skeletons at once victorious and weeping. It was neither the first nor the last time – after Oscar Wilde, Baudelaire, and Poe, after so many, many others – that a subversive artist, a "madman," an undesirable, had become the pride of the very nation which had despised him. "The people" is quick to seize on a new name to worship, totally indifferent to what that name stands for. So the modern state turns its "bad boys" into demigods, mounting and stuffing them for exhibition.

ENSOR AND CONTEMPORARY PAINTING

To situate Ensor properly in the history of art, we must disregard the date of his death, and think of him as a painter of the end of the last century. The significant part of his work had been created by 1900. His case resembles that of Rimbaud, whose entire contribution to literature was made long before he died. It is a gross, though a common, error to set Ensor's work beside that of Matisse, Vuillard, or Kokoschka. His famous *Entry of Christ into Brussels*, (pp. 181, 274, 275), painted in 1888 anticipates by twenty years Matisse's *Dance*, Bonnard's *Paradise*, and Rouault's *Faubourg of Long Suffering*. It was already in existence when Toulouse-Lautrec painted his murals for La Goulue, when Van Gogh painted his *Berceuses*, Gauguin his *Where Do We Come From? What Are We? Where Are We Going?*, and Seurat his *Parade*. Renoir had not as yet painted *Two Girls at the Piano*. Like Cézanne, Gauguin, Van Gogh, Seurat, and Redon, Ensor belongs to the heroic epoch when the Impressionism of Monet, Pissarro, and Sisley was being transcended, and painting left the beaten track of representational reality to penetrate once and for all into the domain of a reality behind ordinary appearances. He helped to forge one of the essential links in the history of painting. He drove out the last remnants of Romanticism, transfigured Realism, dissected, boned, and denaturalized Impressionism, paving the way for an art of heightened color, intenser expression, the gratuitous, the dream – that is, to Fauvism, Expressionism, Dadaism, and Surrealism. With his taste for variety, his anticonformism, his use of previously created works, his repeated abrupt shifts of style, he anticipated at the end of the last century what Picasso was to do at the beginning of this century. The year 1900 was pivotal for both of them. This was the year the torch of genius passed from the older to the younger, when the Fleming had finished his work and the Spaniard was just beginning his. But the former worked in a climate of disapproval, while the latter was quickly to gain recognition.

Baffling in the diversity of his styles, Ensor had no direct continuator anywhere.

Moreover, he had none of the virtues of the teacher, although he had all the virtues of the awakener. He was endowed with the spirit of freedom, the one power that can transform everything. This was how he could pave the way for the innovators who came after him. Almost all of them claimed him as spiritual ancestor, from Rik Wouters to Edgard Tytgat, from Leon Spilliaert to Léon Thevenet, from Constant Permeke to Fritz van den Berghe, from Hippolyte Daeye to Gustave de Smet and Jean Brusselmans.

In his own country he remains the greatest painter since Peter Paul Rubens and Anthony Van Dyck, a revolutionary continuator of Bosch, Mandijn, and Teniers, the spiritual father of a whole phalanx of talented artists. In his own epoch, he remains, with Toulouse-Lautrec, Van Gogh, Rousseau, Munch, and a few others, a painter who powerfully defined the sensibility of his age and inaugurated a spirit of irreverence for reality, which was to leave a deep impress on the twentieth century. In the perspective of the history of art as a whole, he was a passionate inventor of new modes of expression, an exceptional visionary, brother to such artists as Grünewald and Goya, a poet of the absurd, a rebellious mind, a tormented spirit, an incorrigible scoffer, a strange and unique example of detachment with respect to man's unfathomable destiny.

SIGNATURES OF JAMES ENSOR

Portrait of a Man (1880), p. 138

Working the Fields (1882), c. c. 72

Forbidding Figure (Portrait of the
Artist's Aunt) (1890), p. 271

Signature under a dedication (1945),
p. 360

Signature written during the reali-
sation of the film *Masques et Visages
de James Ensor* (1948)

Villa Albert (1876)

Ostend Rooftops - Dächer von Ostende - I tetti di Ostenda (1877)

Bathing Cabin – Strandkabine – Cabina sulla spiaggia (c. 1877)

Model – Das Modell – La modella (1877)

Judas Flinging Pieces of Silver into the Temple – Judas schleudert die Silberlinge in den Tempel
Giuda butta i danari nel tempio (1880)

Triumphal Chariot – Triumphwagen – Carro di trionfo (1877)

Judith and Holofernes – Judith und Holofernes – Giuditta e Oloferne (1878)

Study of Light (Adam and Eve Driven from Paradise) – Lichtstudie (Die Vertreibung aus dem Paradies) – Studio
di luce (Adamo ed Eva cacciati dal Paradiso) (1887)

Sketch for Bourgeois Salon – Skizze für den Bürgerlichen Salon – Schizzo per il Salotto borghese (1880)

Woman with Red Scarf – Dame mit rotem Schal – La signora con lo scialle rosso (1880)

Woman with Blue Scarf – Frau mit blauem Schal – La donna con lo scialle blu (1881)

Portrait of the Artist's Mother – Portrait der Mutter Ensors – Ritratto della madre (1882)

Portrait of Dario de Regoyos – Portrait Dario de Regoyos – Ritratto di Dario de Regoyos (1884)

Portrait of Willy Finch – Portrait Willy Finch – Ritratto di Willy Finch (1882)

Bourgeois Salon – Bürgerlicher Salon – Salotto borghese (1881)

Russian Music – Russische Musik – La musica russa (1881)

Waiting – Die Erwartung – L'attesa (1882)

The Painter and his Model – Der Maler und sein Modell – Il pittore e il suo modello (c. 1880)

In the Woods – Im Wald – Nel bosco (c. 1880)

Ostend Rooftops – Dächer von Ostende – I tetti di Ostenda (1884)

The Colorist – Die Koloristin – La colorista (1880)

Woman in Blue – Dame in Blau – La signora in blu (1881)

Woman Eating Oysters – Die Austernesserin – Donna che mangia le ostriche (1882)

Woman Eating Oysters – Die Austernesserin – Donna che mangia le ostriche (c. 1907)

Pears – Birnen – Pere (1881)

Triptych – Triptychon – Trittico (c. 1880)

Oysters – Austern – Ostriche (1882)

The Skate – Der Rochen – La razza (1882)

The Cab – Die Droschke – La carrozza (c. 1880)

Sick Tramp Warming Himself – Mißmutiger Strolch am Ofen – Pidocchioso malato che si scalda (1882)

Lady in Distress – Die verzweifelte Dame – La signora angosciata (1882)

Children Dressing – Kinder bei der Toilette – La toeletta dei bambini (1886)

Child with Doll – Das Mädchen mit der Puppe – Fanciulla con la bambola (1884)

Flowers in a Bucket or Fanfare in Red – Blumen in einem Eimer oder Rote Fanfare – Fiori in un secchio o Fanfara rossa (1885)

Interior (The Rousseau Drawing Room, Rue Vautier) – Interieur (Der Salon der Rousseaus in der Rue Vautier) – Interno (Il salotto Rousseau in rue Vautier) (1884)

The Embroiderer – Die Stickerin – La ricamatrice (1890)

Portrait of Eugène Demolder – Portrait Eugène Demolder – Ritratto di Eugène Demolder (1893)

Forbidding Figure – Die Griesgrämige – Figura arcigna (1890)

Boats – Boote – Barche (1890)

Boats on the Beach – Boote am Strand – Barche in secca (1900)

The Entry of Christ into Brussels – Christi Einzug in Brüssel – L'ingresso di Cristo a Bruxelles (1888)

Ostend Rooftops – Dächer von Ostende – I tetti di Ostenda (1885)

Hôtel de Ville, Brussels – Das Rathaus in Brüssel – Il municipio di Bruxelles (1885)

The Skate – Der Rochen – La razza (1892)

Curly Cabbage – Wirsingkohl – Il cavolo riccio (1892)

Egg, Crab, and Shrimps, or The Soft-boiled Egg – Ei, Krabben und Krebse oder Das gekochte Ei – Uovo, gamberi
e granchi o L'uovo alla coque (1891)

Still Life with Blue Pot – Stilleben mit blauer Kanne – Natura morta con brocca blu (1890)

Still Life – Stilleben – Natura morta (1893)

Still Life – Stilleben – Natura morta (1890)

People Sticking Out Their Tongues – Die Zungen – Le lingue (c. 1890)

Garden of Love – Der Liebesgarten – Il giardino d'amore (1891)

Andromeda – Andromeda – Andromeda (1925)

Strange Masks – Seltsame Masken – Strane maschere (1892)

Scandalized Masks – Verärgerte Masken – Le maschere scandalizzate (1883)

Baptism with Masks – Maskentaufe – Il battesimo delle maschere (1891)
Masquerade – Maskerade – Mascherata (1891)

Monsieur and Madame Ernest Rousseau talking with Sophie Yoteko – Herr und Frau Rousseau unterhalten sich mit Sophie Yoteko – Il signore e la signora Rousseau s'intrattengono con Sofia Yoteko (1892)

Masks Watching a Turtle – Masken betrachten eine Schildkröte – Maschere che guardano una tartaruga (1894)

The Dangerous Cooks – Die gefährlichen Köche – I cuochi pericolosi (1896)

Murder – Der Mord – L'assassinio (1891)

Masks Confronting Death – Masken begegnen dem Tod – Le maschere davanti alla morte (1888)

Gathering of Skeletons – Die Versammlung der Skelette – Riunione di scheletri (1894)

Badgered Pierrot – Der gepeinigte Pierrot – Pierrot tormentato (1900)

Duel of Masks – Duell der Masken – Duello di maschere (1892)

293

Pierrot and Skeleton in Yellow Robe – Pierrot und Skelett in gelbem Gewand – Pierrot e lo scheletro in giallo (1893)

Skeletons in the Studio – Skelette im Atelier – Scheletri nello studio (1900)

Chinoiseries – Chinoiserien – Cineserie (1907)

Masks – Masken – Maschere (1925)

Ensor with Palette – Ensor mit Palette – Ensor con la tavolozza (c. 1937)

CLASSIFIED CATALOGUE
GRUPPENKATALOG
CATALOGO ILLUSTRATO

PORTRAITS AND FIGURES
PORTRAITS UND GESTALTEN
RITRATTI E FIGURE

1 Girl with the Turned-Up Nose
  Die Frau mit der Stupsnase
  La donna col naso all'insù
  1879

2 The Painter Willy Finch on the Dunes
  Der Maler Willy Finch in den Dünen
  Il pittore Willy Finch fra le dune
  1880

3 Portrait of Mme. Ernest Rousseau
  Portrait Mme. Ernest Rousseau
  Ritratto della signora Rousseau
  1880

4 The Painter Willy Finch (or Vogels)
  in His Studio
  Der Maler Willy Finch (oder Vogels)
  in seinem Atelier
  Il pittore Willy Finch (o Vogels)
  nel suo studio
  1880

5 Head of the Painter Willy Finch
  Kopf des Malers Willy Finch
  Testa del pittore Willy Finch
  1880

6 Wool-Carder
  Der Wollkämmer
  Il cardatore
  1881

7 The Painter Willy Finch
  Der Maler Willy Finch
  Il pittore Willy Finch
  1882

8 Lady with Red Umbrella
  Dame mit rotem Sonnenschirm
  La signora con parasole rosso
  1882

9 Portrait of Théo Hannon
  Portrait Théo Hannon
  Ritratto di Théo Hannon
  1882

10 The Antiquary
   Der Antiquar
   L'antiquario
   1902

11 Lady in Blue
   Dame in Blau
   Signora in azzurro
   1906

12 Portrait of Mme. Emma Lambotte
   Portrait Mme. Emma Lambotte
   Ritratto della signora Emma Lambotte
   1907

13 Droll Smokers (Augusta Boogaerts and
   the painter Willem Paerels)
   Drollige Raucher (Augusta Boogaerts
   und der Maler Willem Paerels)
   Fumatori scherzosi (Augusta Boogaerts
   e il pittore Willem Paerels)
   1920

14 Portrait of Mme. C.
   Portrait Mme. C.
   Ritratto della signora C.
   1927

15 Portrait of Monsieur X.
   Portrait Monsieur X.
   Ritratto del signor X.
   1928

16 Portrait of Carol Deutsch
   Portrait Carol Deutsch
   Ritratto di Carol Deutsch
   1928

17 Lady Resting (Augusta Boogaerts)
  Ruhende Dame (Augusta Boogaerts)
  Signora che riposa (Augusta Boogaerts)
  c. 1930

18 Portrait of Mlle. Augusta Boogaerts
  Portrait Mlle. Augusta Boogaerts
  Ritratto della signorina Augusta
  Boogaerts
  c. 1930

SELF-PORTRAITS
SELBSTPORTRAITS
AUTORITRATTI

19 Self-Portrait
  Selbstportrait
  Autoritratto
  1879

20 Self-Portrait
  Selbstportrait
  Autoritratto
  1879

21 Self-Portrait (replica of 1879 painting)
  Selbstportrait (Replik eines Bildes
  von 1879)
  Autoritratto (copia di un dipinto del
  1879)
  c. 1923

22 Portrait of the Painter in a Flowered Hat
  Ensor mit dem Blumenhut
  Ensor col cappello infiorato
  1883

23 Self-Portrait
  Selbstportrait
  Autoritratto
  1883

24 Sheet of Self-Portrait sketches
  Blatt mit Selbstportrait-Skizzen
  Pagina con schizzi di autoritratto
  c. 1885

25 My Portrait Skeletonized
Mein Portrait als Skelett
Il mio ritratto come scheletro
1889

26 Self-Portrait
Selbstportrait
Autoritratto
c. 1890

27 Self-Portrait
Selbstportrait
Autoritratto
c. 1895

28 Self-Portrait
Selbstportrait
Autoritratto
c. 1905

29 Self-Portrait
Selbstportrait
Autoritratto
1929

30 Ensor Surrounded by Masks
Ensor von Masken umgeben
Ensor attorniato da maschere
c. 1930

31 Ensor the Musician in the Key of G
Ensor als Musikant mit dem Violin-
schlüssel
Ensor musicante in chiave di sol
1939

SHIPS AND HARBORS
SCHIFFE UND HÄFEN
BARCHE E PORTI

32 Boats at the Docks
   Boote am Pfahlwerk
   Barche presso l'ormeggio
   c. 1873

33 Shrimp Fishers
   Krabbenfischer
   Pescatori di granchi
   c. 1878

34 Boat Aground, La Panne
   Gestrandetes Boot, La Panne
   Barca in secca, La Panne
   1876

35 Boat Aground, La Panne
   Gestrandetes Boot, La Panne
   Barca in secca, La Panne
   c. 1925

36 Seascape
   Seestück
   Marina
   c. 1878

37 Boats
   Boote
   Battelli
   1886

38 The Harbor of Ostend
   Der Hafen von Ostende
   Il porto di Ostenda
   1888

39 Boats
   Boote
   Battelli
   1888

40 Ostend
   Ostende
   Ostenda
   c. 1890

41 The Basin at Ostend
   Das Hafenbecken von Ostende
   Il bacino di Ostenda
   1890

42 The Canal
   Der Kanal
   Il canale
   1902

43 The Canal
   Der Kanal
   Il canale
   c. 1930

DUNES AND BEACH
DÜNEN UND STRAND
DUNE E SPIAGGIA

44 Pole in the Dunes
   Pfahl in den Dünen
   Palo nelle dune
   1876

45 Pole in the Dunes
   Pfahl in den Dünen
   Palo nelle dune
   1876

46 Dunes, Sea, and Ships
   Dünen, Meer und Schiffe
   Dune, mare e battelli
   1876

47 Dunes, Sea, and Ships
   Dünen, Meer und Schiffe
   Dune, mare e battelli
   c. 1935

48 Landscape, Dunes
   Landschaft mit Dünen
   Paesaggio con dune
   1876

49 Dunes
   Dünen
   Dune
   1876

50 Dunes
   Dünen
   Dune
   1876

51 Buoys on the Beach
   Bojen auf dem Strand
   Salvagenti sulla spiaggia
   c. 1878

52 Lighthouse at Ostend
   Der Leuchtturm von Ostende
   Il faro di Ostenda
   1885

53 Dunes and Calm Sea
   Dünen und stilles Meer
   Dune e mare calmo
   c. 1885

54 The Beach
   Der Strand
   La spiaggia
   c. 1910

THE SEA
DAS MEER
IL MARE

55 Seascape
Seestück
Marina
1877

56 Calm Sea (or Bright Seascape)
Stilles Meer (oder Helles Seestück)
Mare calmo (o Marina chiara)
1880 (dated on the back 1877, auf der
Rückseite datiert 1877, datato sul retro
1877)

57 The Breakwater
Der Wellenbrecher
La diga
1882

58 Sunset over the Sea
Sonnenuntergang auf dem Meer
Tramonto sul mare
1885

59 The White Cloud
Die weiße Wolke
La nuvola bianca
1882

60 Gray Sea
Graues Meer
Mare grigio
1880

61 Seascape
Seestück
Marina
c. 1882

62 Seascape
Seestück
Marina
c. 1915

LANDSCAPES I (without
houses or figures)
LANDSCHAFTEN I
(ohne Häuser oder Figuren)
PAESAGGI I
(senza case o figure)

63 Pond with Poplars (or Park at Ostend)
Teich mit Pappeln (oder Der Park von
Ostende)
Lo stagno dei pioppi (o Il parco
di Ostenda)
1880

64 Stream in the Woods
Bach im Walde
Ruscello nel bosco
1880

65 Wind
Der Windstoß
Colpo di vento sulla siepe
1888

66 The Domain of Arnheim
Die Domäne von Arnheim
La proprietà di Arnheim
1890

LANDSCAPES II
(with houses or figures)
LANDSCHAFTEN II
(mit Häusern oder Figuren)
PAESAGGI II
(con case o figure)

67 The Flemish Plain Seen from the Dunes
Flämische Ebene, von den Dünen ge-
sehen
La pianura fiamminga vista dalle dune
1876

68 Estaminet
Kneipe
La bettola
1877

69 Outskirts of Blankenberghe
Umgebung von Blankenberghe
I dintorni di Blankenberghe
c. 1877

70 Water Gate near Ostend
Großer Damm bei Ostende
La grande diga nei pressi di Ostenda
c. 1878

71 Landscape with Church (after Constable)
   Landschaft mit Kirche (nach Constable)
   Paesaggio con chiesa (da Constable)
   c. 1880

72 Working the Fields
   Feldarbeit
   Lavori nei campi
   1882

73 Cottages on the Dunes
   Häuser in den Dünen
   Casette fra le dune
   1882

74 Landscape
   Landschaft
   Paesaggio
   1886

75 The Large View of Mariakerke
   Ansicht von Mariakerke
   Veduta di Mariakerke
   1887

76 The Tower of Lisseweghe
   Der Turm von Lisseweghe
   La torre di Lisseweghe
   1888

77 Path at Groenendael
   Fußweg bei Groenendael
   Sentiero a Groenendael
   1888

78 View of Mariakerke
   Ansicht von Mariakerke
   Veduta di Mariakerke
   1901

STREETS AND HOUSES
STRASSEN UND HÄUSER
STRADE E CASE

79 Street at Ostend
   Straße in Ostende
   Una strada di Ostenda
   1882

80 Hôtel de Ville, Oudenaarde
   Das Rathaus in Oudenaarde
   Il municipio di Oudenaarde
   1888

81 The Street Lamp
   Die Straßenlaterne
   Il lampione
   1888

82 View of Ostend
   Ansicht von Ostende
   Veduta di Ostenda
   1889

83 Street at Ostend
   Straße in Ostende
   Una strada di Ostenda
   1890

84 Ostend Rooftops
   Die Dächer von Ostende
   I tetti di Ostenda
   1906

85 Avenue de la Chasse, Brussels
   Avenue de la Chasse, Brüssel
   Avenue de la Chasse, Bruxelles
   c. 1938

86 Avenue de la Chasse, Brussels
   Avenue de la Chasse, Brüssel
   Avenue de la Chasse, Bruxelles
   c. 1938

INTERIORS
INTERIEURS
INTERNI

87 The Stove
Der Ofen
La stufa
1880

88 My Favorite Room
Mein Lieblingszimmer
La mia camera prediletta
1892

89 The Studio of the Artist
Das Atelier des Künstlers
Lo studio dell'artista
c. 1930

90 Interior with Three Portraits
Interieur mit drei Portraits
Interno con tre ritratti
1938

STILL LIFES I
STILLEBEN I
NATURE MORTE I

91 Chinese screen
Chinesischer Paravent
Il paravento cinese
c. 1880

92 Still Life
Stilleben
Natura morta
c. 1880

93 Chair with Fan
Stuhl mit Fächer
Sedia con ventaglio
1880

94 Blue and Pink Drapery
Blaue und rosa Stoffe
Drappi azzurri e rosa
1880

95 Still Life with Blue Chinoiseries
  Stilleben mit blauen Chinoiserien
  Natura morta con cineserie azzurre
  1880

96 Still Life
  Stilleben
  Natura morta
  c. 1891

97 Bric-à-Brac
  Trödelkram
  Cianfrusaglie
  1896

98 Still Life with Chinoiseries
  Stilleben mit Chinoiserien
  Natura morta con cineserie
  c. 1907

99 Still Life with Lantern
  Stilleben mit Laterne
  Natura morta con lanterna
  1910

100 Delicacy
  Leckerbissen
  Leccornie
  c. 1925

101 Still Life with China Figurine and Pipe
  Stilleben mit Chinesen und Pfeife
  Natura morta con cinese e pipa
  1915

STILL LIFES II
(Fruit, Vegetables, Fish, etc.)
STILLEBEN II
(Früchte, Gemüse, Fisch usw.)
NATURE MORTE II
(Frutta, ortaggi, pesce, ecc.)

102 Still Life
Stilleben
Natura morta
1880

103 Apples
Äpfel
Mele
1880

104 Curly Cabbage
Wirsingkohl
Il cavolo riccio
1880

105 Curly Cabbage
Wirsingkohl
Il cavolo riccio
c. 1893

106 Meats
Fleischwaren
Carni
1881

107 Seashells and Chinoiseries
Muscheln und Chinoiserien
Conchiglie e cineserie
1882

108 Still Life: The Hare
Stilleben: Der Hase
Natura morta: La lepre
1885

109 Small Fruits
Kleine Früchte
Piccoli frutti
1889

110 Still Life
   Stilleben
   Natura morta
   c. 1893

111 Shrimp
   Krabben
   Gamberi
   1894

112 Fish
   Fische
   Pesci
   1895

113 Flowers and Vegetables
   Blumen und Gemüse
   Fiori e ortaggi
   1896

114 Seashells and Fish
   Muscheln und Fische
   Conchiglie e pesci
   1898

115 Still Life with Duck
   Stilleben mit Ente
   Natura morta con anitra
   1910

116 Still Life with Fruits
   Stilleben mit Früchten
   Natura morta con frutta
   c. 1910

117 Still Life with Cabbage
   Stilleben mit Kohl
   Natura morta con cavolo
   1921

118 Red Cabbage
    Rotkohl
    Il cavolo rosso
    1925

119 Seashells
    Muscheln
    Conchiglie
    c. 1931

120 Flowers, Fruits, and Sniffing Masks
    Blumen, Früchte und Schnüfflermasken
    Fiori, frutta e maschere che annusano
    1935

FLOWERS
BLUMEN
FIORI

121 Flowers and Fruits
    Blumen und Früchte
    Fiori e frutta
    c. 1889

122 Flowers
    Blumen
    Fiori
    1892

123 Flowers
    Blumen
    Fiori
    c. 1909

124 Azaleas
    Azaleen
    Azalee
    c. 1900

125 Flowers and Masks
   Blumen und Masken
   Fiori e maschere
   c. 1928

126 Dahlias
   Dahlien
   Dalie
   c. 1930

MASKS AND SKELETONS
MASKEN UND SKELETTE
MASCHERE E SCHELETRI

127 Haunted Furniture
   Das Spukmöbel
   Il mobile stregato
   1885

128 The Artist Decomposed
   Der Maler in Verwesung
   Il pittore decomposto
   1886

129 Old Woman with Masks
   Die Alte mit den Masken
   La vecchia con le maschere
   1889

130 Skeletons Fighting for the Body of a
   Hanged Man
   Masken im Streit um einen Gehenkten
   Scheletri che si contendono un impiccato
   1891

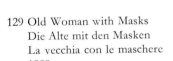

131 Masks Confronting Death
   Die Masken und der Tod
   Le maschere davanti alla morte
   c. 1890

132 The Despair of Pierrot
   Die Verzweiflung des Pierrot
   La disperazione di Pierrot
   c. 1915 (back-dated 1892, rückdatiert
   1892, predatato 1892)

133 Skeleton Musicians
    Musizierende Skelette
    Scheletri musicanti
    1908

134 Intrige
    Die Intrige
    L'intrigo
    1911

135 Figures in Front of a Poster for the
    "Game of Love"
    Figuren vor dem Plakat der »Liebes-
    Tonleiter«
    Persone davanti al manifesto di
    «La gamme d'amour»
    1914

136 Carnival
    Karneval
    Carnevale
    c. 1920

137 Masks
    Masken
    Maschere
    1922

138 Masks
    Masken
    Maschere
    c. 1927

139 You are Masks!
    Masken seid ihr!
    Maschere voi siete!
    1924

140 Banquet of the Starved
    Das Bankett der Hungernden
    Il banchetto degli affamati
    c. 1925

141 The Stranger
   Der Fremde
   Lo straniero
   c. 1930

142 Mona Lisa among Masks
   Mona Lisa unter den Masken
   Monna Lisa fra le maschere
   c. 1931

HISTORY, PAST AND PRESENT
GESCHICHTE, VERGANGENHEIT
UND GEGENWART
STORIA, PASSATO E PRESENTE

143 Napoleon at Waterloo
   Napoleon bei Waterloo
   Napoleone a Waterloo
   1890

144 Remorse of the Corsican Ogre
   Gewissensbisse des korsischen Men-
   schenfressers
   Rimorsi dell'orco corso
   c. 1890

145 Fishermen's Strike at Ostend
   (or Gendarmes firing at Fishermen)
   Streik der Fischer in Ostende
   (oder Gendarmen feuern auf Fischer)
   Lo sciopero dei pescatori a Ostenda
   (o I gendarmi sparano sui pescatori)
   c. 1892

146 The Strike
   Der Streik
   Lo sciopero
   1892

147 The Germans in Belgium (1914–18)
   Die Deutschen in Belgien (1914–18)
   I tedeschi in Belgio (1914–18)
   c. 1914

148 The Germans in Belgium (1914–18)
   Die Deutschen in Belgien (1914–18)
   I tedeschi in Belgio (1914–18)
   c. 1914

SATIRE AND POLEMIC
SATIRE UND POLEMIK
SATIRA E POLEMICA

149 Peste dessous, peste dessus, peste partout
   Pest unten, Pest oben, Pest überall
   Peste sotto, peste sopra, peste dappertutto
   1889

150 Philip II in Hell
   Philipp II. in der Hölle
   Filippo II all'inferno
   1891

151 The Dispute
   Der Disput
   La disputa
   1895

152 Study for "Envy"
   Studie zu »Der Neid«
   Studio per «L'invidia»
   1902

153 Study for "Envy"
   Studie zu »Der Neid«
   Studio per «L'invidia»
   1902

154 Infamous Vivisectors
   Die niederträchtigen Vivisekteure
   Gli infami vivisettori
   1925

155 Physicians Belaboring a Fat Girl
   Ärzte »kurieren« eine schwangere Frau
   Medici che hanno in cura una ragazza
   incinta
   1926

FANTASIES, GROTESQUES,
LEGENDS, AND TALES
PHANTASIEN, GROTESKEN,
LEGENDEN UND ERZÄHLUNGEN
FANTASIE, STORIE GROTTESCHE,
LEGGENDE E RACCONTI

156 Roman Triumph
   Triumph der Römer
   Trionfo romano
   c. 1889

157 Battle of the Golden Spurs
   Die Schlacht der goldenen Sporen
   La battaglia degli Speroni d'oro
   1891

158 The Rout of the Mercenaries
   Fliehende Haudegen
   Masnadieri in rotta
   1892

159 The Elephants' Ball
   Tanz der Elefanten
   Il ballo degli elefanti
   1892

160 Cruel Joke on the Peasants
   Die gefoppten Bauern
   Contadini turlupinati
   c. 1896

161 The Massacre of the Innocents
   Die Hinmetzelung der Unschuldigen
   La strage degli innocenti
   1913

162 Combat
   Der Kampf
   Il combattimento
   c. 1910

163 War of the Snails
   Der Krieg der Schnecken
   La guerra delle lumache
   1913

164 Delights of Winter
   Winterfreuden
   I piaceri dell'inverno
   1914

165 Moses and the Birds
   Moses und die Vögel
   Mosé e gli uccelli
   1924

166 The Deliverance of Andromeda
   Die Befreiung der Andromeda
   La liberazione d'Andromeda
   c. 1925

167 Lady Godiva
   Lady Godiva
   Lady Godiva
   c. 1930

168 Priapus Caressed
   Zärtlichkeit für Priapus
   Carezza a Priapo
   c. 1932

THEATER AND BALLET
THEATER UND BALLETT
TEATRO E BALLETTO

169 Ballet Dancers
   Die Ballerinen
   Le ballerine
   1895

170 Ballet Dancers
   Die Ballerinen
   Le ballerine
   1908

171 Theater of Masks
   Das Maskentheater
   Il teatro delle maschere
   1889

172 Small Theater
   Kleines Theater
   Teatrino
   1914

173 Queen of the Ballet with Wreath of
   Flowers
   Ballettkönigin mit Blumenkranz
   La regina del balletto con ghirlande di
   fiori
   1930

174 Queen of the Ballet
   Ballettkönigin
   La regina del balletto
   1930

175 The Dance of Daisies
   Ballerinen als Margeriten
   Il ballo delle margherite
   c. 1935

THE GAME OF LOVE
DIE LIEBES-TONLEITER
LA GAMME D'AMOUR

176 Fifrelin (figure for "The Game of Love")
   Fifrelin (Figurine für: Die Liebes-
   Tonleiter)
   Fifrelin (figurino per «La gamme
   d'amour»)
   1911

177 Brutonne (figure for "The Game of
   Love")
   Brutonne (Figurine für: Die Liebes-
   Tonleiter)
   Brutonne (figurino per «La gamme
   d'amour»)
   1911

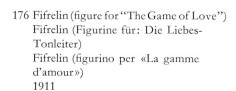

178 Miami (figure for "The Game of Love")
   Miami (Figurine für: Die Liebes-
   Tonleiter)
   Miami (figurino per «La gamme
   d'amour»)
   1911

179 Decor for "The Game of Love"
   (2nd Act)
   Dekoration für: Die Liebes-Tonleiter
   (2. Akt)
   Bozzetto scenico per «La gamme
   d'amour» (atto II)
   1914

180 Decor for "The Game of Love"
   Dekoration für: Die Liebes-
   Tonleiter
   Bozzetto scenico per «La gamme
   d'amour»
   1914

181 Unmasked
   Die abgerissene Maske
   La maschera strappata
   1915

THE GARDEN OF LOVE, NUDES
DER LIEBESGARTEN,
AKTDARSTELLUNGEN
IL GIARDINO D'AMORE, NUDI

182 Garden of Love
   Der Liebesgarten
   Il giardino d'amore
   1888

183 Bathers, Undulating Lines
   Badende, Kurven- und Wellenlinien
   Bagnanti, linee curve e ondulate
   1916

184 Little Gathering in a Park
   Kleine Gesellschaft im Park
   Piccola riunione in un parco
   c. 1910

185 Little Gathering in a Park
   Kleine Gesellschaft im Park
   Piccola riunione in un parco
   c. 1920

186 Bird Park
   Parkszene
   Scena nel parco
   c. 1925

187 Seashells and Mollusks
   Muscheln und Mollusken
   Conchiglie e molluschi
   c. 1925

BIBLE, RELIGION
BIBEL, RELIGION
LA BIBBIA, LA RELIGIONE

188 Susanna and the Elders
   Susanna im Bade
   Susanna e i vecchioni
   1882

189 The Cruel: Jesus Presented to the
   People
   Jesus wird dem Volke gezeigt
   Gesù presentato al popolo
   1885

190 Calvary
   Die Kreuzigung
   Calvario
   1886

191 The Dead Christ Watched Over by the
   Angels
   Christus von Engeln bewacht
   Cristo vegliato dagli angeli
   1886

192 The Adoration of the Shepherds
   Die Anbetung der Hirten
   L'adorazione dei pastori
   1886

193 The Adoration of the Shepherds
   Die Anbetung der Hirten
   L'adorazione dei pastori
   1887

194 Christ Mocked
   Die Verspottung Christi
   Cristo deriso
   1892

195 Joan of Arc
   Jeanne d'Arc
   Giovanna d'Arco
   1892

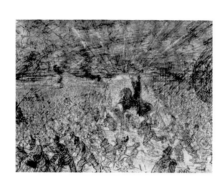

196 Consoling Virgin
   Die trostreiche Jungfrau
   La Vergine consolatrice
   1892

197 Joshua Comments the Sun
   Josua befiehlt der Sonne
   Giosué comanda al sole
   c. 1892

198 Project for a Chapel dedicated to Saints
   Peter and Paul
   Entwurf für eine St. Peter und Paul ge-
   weihte Kapelle
   Progetto di cappella dedicata ai
   S.S. Pietro e Paolo
   1897

199 The Virgin of Sorrows
   Die schmerzensreiche Muttergottes
   La Vergine dei dolori
   1904

200 The Annunciation
   Die Verkündigung
   L'annunciazione
   1912

201 Procession of the Penitents at Furnes
   Prozession der Büßer von Furnes
   Processione dei penitenti di Furnes
   1913

202 Jesus Among the Doctors
Jesus vor den Schriftgelehrten
Gesù fra i dottori
1920

203 Christ
Christus
Cristo
1925

204 The Temptation of St. Anthony
Die Versuchung des Heiligen Antonius
La tentazione di Sant'Antonio
1927

205 The Procession of St. Godelieve at
Ghistelles
St. Godelieve-Prozession in Ghistelles
La processione di S. Godelieve a
Ghistelles
1939

PORTRAIT STUDIES AND
FIGURE SKETCHES
PORTRAITSTUDIEN UND
FIGÜRLICHE SKIZZEN
STUDI DI RITRATTI E
SCHIZZI DI FIGURE

206 Young Sailor
Junger Seemann
Giovane marinaio
1880

207 Ostend Boy
Ostender Type
Tipo di Ostenda
1880

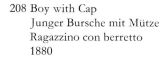

208 Boy with Cap
Junger Bursche mit Mütze
Ragazzino con berretto
1880

209 Seated Man
Sitzender Mann
Uomo seduto
1880

210 Man Reading
Der Lesende
Uomo che legge
1880

211 Maidservant
Die Magd
La serva
1880

212 Boy
Der Junge
Il monello
1880

213 Seated Boy
Sitzender Junge
Monello seduto
1880

214 Head of a Woman
Frauenkopf
Testa di donna
c. 1882

215 Sleeping Woman
Eingeschlafene Frau
Donna addormentata
c. 1882

216 The Artist's Sister
Die Schwester des Künstlers
La sorella dell'artista
c. 1883

217 Sleep (sheet of studies)
Schlaf (Studienblatt)
Il sonno (studio)
c. 1883

218 Portrait
   Portrait
   Ritratto
   c. 1883

219 Child Drawing
   Zeichnendes Kind
   Fanciullo che disegna
   c. 1883

DRAWINGS AFTER OTHER
MASTERS
ZEICHNUNGEN NACH
ANDEREN MEISTERN
DISEGNI ISPIRATI AD ALTRI
ARTISTI

220 Study (after Watteau)
   Studie (nach Watteau)
   Studio (da Watteau)
   1877

221 Troop of Soldiers (after Callot)
   Soldatentrupp (nach Callot)
   Truppa di militari (da Callot)
   c. 1878

222 Sketch (after Goya)
   Skizze (nach Goya)
   Schizzo (da Goya)
   c. 1878

223 Dog (after Rembrandt)
   Hund (nach Rembrandt)
   Cane (da Rembrandt)
   c. 1880

224 Page from a sketchbook
   Seite eines Skizzenheftes
   Pagina di un quaderno di schizzi
   c. 1880

225 Page from a sketchbook
   Seite eines Skizzenheftes
   Pagina di un quaderno di schizzi
   c. 1880

226 Portrait (after Frans Hals)
Portrait (nach Frans Hals)
Ritratto (da Frans Hals)
c. 1880

227 Study
Studie
Studio
c. 1880

SKETCHES
SKIZZEN
SCHIZZI

228 Fiacre in Front of the Theater at Ostend
Kutsche vor dem Theater in Ostende
Carrozza davanti al teatro di Ostenda
c. 1880

229 The Cart
Der Karren
Il carretto
c. 1880

230 Sketch with Fisherman's Lantern
Zeichnung mit Fischerlampe
Disegno con una lampada da pescatore
c. 1880

231 Umbrella
Regenschirm
L'ombrello
c. 1883

232 Figures
Zeittypen
Tipi dell'epoca
1880

233 Female Silhouettes
Weibliche Silhouetten
Figure femminili
c. 1880

234 Figures
    Figuren
    Figure
    c. 1880

235 Hunters in Winter
    Jäger im Winter
    Cacciatori in inverno
    1881

236 Sketch
    Skizze
    Schizzo
    c. 1880

MISCELLANEOUS
VERSCHIEDENES
SOGGETTI VARI

237 Plate in Embossed Leather
    Tablett aus Leder
    Quadro di cuoio bulinato
    c. 1900

238 Don Quixote
    Don Quijote
    Don Chisciotte
    c. 1885

239 The Lamp Boy
    Der Lampenjunge
    Il lampionaio
    c. 1920

240 Sick Tramp Warming Himself
    Mißmutiger Strolch am Ofen
    Pidocchioso malato che si scalda
    c. 1925 (back-dated 1910, rückdatiert
    1910, predatato 1910)

DOCUMENTS
DOKUMENTARISCHER TEIL
DOCUMENTI FOTOGRAFICI

Self-Portrait *(later titled* My Portrait Sad and Sumptuous) – Selbstportrait *(später betitelt* Mein Portrait in Trauer und Prunk) – Autoritratto *(più tardi intitolato* Il mio ritratto triste e sontuoso) (1886)

Demons tormenting Me – Dämonen, die mich quälen – Diavoli che mi beffano (1888)

Ensor, who liked the theme of this drawing, used it in 1895 in an etching (see p. 124), and in 1898 in a lithograph which served as poster for the exhibition of his works organized by "La Plume", and after 1900, for several small paintings.

Ensor, dem das Thema sehr am Herzen lag, benutzte diese Zeichnung 1895 für eine Radierung (siehe S. 124), 1898 für eine Lithographie, die als Plakat für die von der Zeitschrift »La Plume« veranstaltete Ausstellung diente, und nach 1900 für mehrere kleine Gemälde.

A questo tema, caro al pittore, s'ispirano anche un' acquaforte del 1895 (v. p. 124), una litografia del 1898 che servì da cartellone per la mostra organizzata da «La Plume», e dopo il 1900, vari quadri di piccolo formato.

Self-Portrait – Selbstportrait – Autoritratto (1883)

At this time the people of Ostend called him "Pietje-de-dood" (the Grim Reaper).

In Ostende wurde Ensor damals »Pietje-de-dood« (Gevatter Tod) genannt.

La gente di Ostenda lo chiamava allora «Pietje-de-dood» (Compare Morte).

Ensor, in a photograph taken in 1883, showing him with wavy hair, a massive nose, a protruding mouth with fleshy lips, and a receding chin that his beard was beginning to conceal.

Eine Photographie Ensors von 1883 zeigt ihn mit welligem Haar, kräftiger Nase, vorgewölbtem Mund, fleischigen Lippen und fliehendem Kinn, das der beginnende Bart zu verbergen suchte.

Una fotografia del 1883 mostra Ensor con i capelli ondulati, il naso grosso, la bocca carnosa, il mento sfuggente già quasi nascosto dalla barba.

337

1 2 3 4

1–4 *Details from self-portraits:* 1 Portrait of the Artist at the Easel (1879). 2 Self-Portrait (1885). 3 In the Shadow (1886). 4 Portrait of the Artist at the Easel (1890).

Ausschnitte von Selbstportraits: 1 Selbstportrait mit Staffelei (1879). 2 Selbstportrait (1885). 3 Im Dunkel (1886). 4 Selbstportrait mit Staffelei (1890).

Particolari dagli autoritratti: 1 Autoritratto davanti al cavalletto (1879). 2 Autoritratto (1885). 3 Nell'ombra (1886). 4 Autoritratto davanti al cavalletto (1890).

5 6

5–6 *Details from self-portraits:* 5 Ensor at the Harmonium (1933). 6 Ensor with Palette (c. 1937).

Ausschnitte von Selbstportraits: 5 Ensor am Harmonium (1933). 6 Ensor mit Palette (c. 1937).

Particolari dagli autoritratti: 5 Ensor all'harmonium (1933). 6 Ensor con la tavolozza (c. 1937).

11 Rubens. Self-Portrait – Selbstportrait – Autoritratto (1623–24)
The detail has been reversed in our reproduction. Seitenverkehrter Ausschnitt. Il particolare è riprodotto invertito.
12 Ensor. Portrait of the Artist Surrounded by Masks – Selbstportrait mit Masken – Autoritratto con maschere (1899)
Detail. Detail. Particolare.

7   8   9   10

7–10 *Details from self-portraits:* 7 Ecce homo or Christ and his Critics (1891). 8 The Dangerous Cooks (1896). 9 Ensor and General Leman Discussing Painting (1890). 10 Consoling Virgin (1892).

Ausschnitte von Selbstportraits: 7 Ecce homo oder Christus und die Kritiker (1891). 8 Die gefährlichen Köche (1896).

9 Ensor und der General Leman diskutieren die Malerei (1890). 10 Die trostreiche Jungfrau (1892).

Particolari dagli autoritratti: 7 Ecce homo o Cristo e i critici (1891). 8 I cuochi pericolosi (1896). 9 Ensor e il generale Leman discutono di pittura (1890). 10 La Vergine consolatrice (1892).

11   12

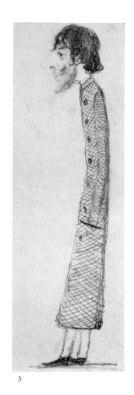

1   2   3

1 Isidore Verheyden. Portrait of James Ensor – Portrait
James Ensor – Ritratto di James Ensor (1886)
2 Rik Wouters. Bust of James Ensor – Portraitbüste
James Ensors – Busto di James Ensor (1913)
*Drawn during one of Ensor's visits to the Rousseaus in Brussels
(1880–1900).*
*Die Zeichnung stammt aus der Zeit der Besuche Ensors bei den
Rousseaus in Brüssel (1880–1900).*
*Il disegno risale al tempo dei soggiorni di Ensor a Bruxelles
(1880–1900).*
3 Ernest Rousseau sen. James Ensor

Gabrielle Bedoret. Ensor in His Studio – Ensor in seinem
Atelier – Ensor nel suo studio (not dated – undatiert –
senza data)
Henry de Groux. Portrait of James Ensor – Portrait
James Ensor – Ritratto di James Ensor (1907)

1

1 Jacques Ochs. Ensor in His Studio – Ensor in seinem Atelier – Ensor nel suo studio (1911)
2 Unknown artist. Ensor in His Studio (not dated)
Unbekannter Maler. Ensor in seinem Atelier (undatiert)
Pittore ignoto. Ensor nel suo studio (senza data)

2

1

2

1 Page of the catalogue of the exhibition of "Les XX" (1888). Each page of the catalogue reproduced the writing and drawing of an exhibiting artist.

Katalog der Ausstellung der »XX« (1888). Jede Seite des Katalogs gibt Schriftzüge und Zeichnungen eines der ausstellenden Künstler wieder.

Catalogo dell'esposizione dei «Venti» (1888). Ogni pagina del catalogo della mostra riproduce autografi e disegni degli artisti espositori.

2 Page from a notebook (after 1929). In the later years of his life Ensor made sketches of his finished paintings in a note book adding commentaries.

Seite eines Skizzenbuches (nach 1929). In späten Jahren nahm Ensor die Gewohnheit an, seine Arbeiten zu skizzieren und mit einem Kommentar zu versehen.

Una pagina da un album di schizzi (dopo il 1929). Negli ultimi anni Ensor prese l'abitudine di fare degli schizzi dei suoi lavori e di postillarli.

3 Ensor in his studio (1933)
Ensor in seinem Atelier (1933)
Ensor nel suo studio (1933)

4 Ensor among his canvases. Photograph taken in 1887 or 1888, of the attic studio, in the house at the corner of the Rue de Flandre and Boulevard Van Iseghem. Facing the artist is a preliminary study of "The Entry of Christ into Brussels" (see pp. 181, 274, 275). On his left we see "Astonishment of the Mask Wouse" (see p. 169).

Ensor zwischen seinen Bildern. Die Aufnahme wurde 1887 oder 1888 in seinem Dachatelier an der Ecke der Rue de Flandre und des Boulevard Van Iseghem gemacht. Vor dem Maler der »Einzug Christi in Brüssel« (siehe S. 181, 274, 275) im Entwurfsstadium, links von ihm die »Verwunderung der Maske Wouse« (siehe S. 169).

Ensor fra i suoi quadri (1887 o 1888). Fotografia presa nella soffitta-studio. Davanti al pittore «L'Ingresso di Cristo a Bruxelles» (v. p. 181, 274–275) allo stato di abbozzo; a sinistra, lo «Stupore della maschera Wouse» (v. p. 169).

3

4

1

2

1 *Excursion to Bruges (1889). From left to right: Ensor; Professor Ernest Rousseau; Willy Finch, painter and ceramist; Mariette Rousseau; "Mitche" Ensor; and Antonio Roiti, professor of physics at the University of Florence. Ensor was inspired by this photograph in executing the drawing and the engraving entitled "Peste dessus, peste dessous, peste partout" (see c.c. 149).*

Reise nach Brügge (1889). Von links nach rechts: Ensor; Professor Ernest Rousseau sen.; der Maler und Keramiker Willy Finch; Mariette Rousseau; »Mitche« Ensor und der Professor für Physik an der Universität Florenz, Antonio Roiti. Die Photographie hat Ensor zu seiner Radierung »Pest unten, Pest oben, Pest überall« (siehe K. 149) angeregt.

In gita a Bruges (1889). Da sinistra a destra: Ensor; Ernest Rousseau padre; il pittore e ceramista Willy Finch; Mariette Rousseau; «Mitche» Ensor e Antonio Roiti, professore di fisica all'Università di Firenze. Questa fotografia ha ispirato il disegno e la stampa intitolati: «Peste sopra, peste sotto, peste dappertutto» (v. C. 149).

2 *Mariette Rousseau, wife of Ernest Rousseau, and Ensor, her protégé. She bought the painter's works and encouraged him when he was depressed. Ensor was inspired by this daguerrotype, taken about 1885, when he made the engraving entitled "Bizarre Little Figures".*

Mariette Rousseau, die Gattin von Ernest Rousseau sen., und Ensor, ihr Schützling. Sie kaufte ihm Bilder ab und stand ihm in Augenblicken der Entmutigung bei. Diese Daguerrotypie von ungefähr 1885 hat Ensor zu seiner Radierung »Kleine bizarre Gestalten« angeregt.

Mariette Rousseau, moglie di Ernest Rousseau padre, e Ensor, suo protetto. Essa gli acquistava opere, lo sosteneva nei momenti di depressione. A questo dagherrotipo del 1895 Ensor si è ispirato per una stampa dal titolo: «Piccole figure bizzarre».

3 *Ensor (c. 1898)*

4 *Ensor in the entrance of 27 Rue de Flandre, the building that has since become the Ensor Museum in Ostend.*

Ensor im Eingang der Rue de Flandre 27, dem Gebäude, das seitdem das Ensor-Museum in Ostende geworden ist.

Ensor sull'ingresso del numero 27 di rue de Flandre. L'edificio divenne poi il Museo Ensor a Ostenda.

5 *The harbor at Ostend*
Der Hafen von Ostende
Il porto di Ostenda

3

4

6 *Ensor in a street at Ostend*
Ensor in einer Ostender Straße
Ensor in una via di Ostenda

7 *The house that Ensor was to inherit from his mater-*
nal uncle (the man with the white beard), and which
he occupied from 1917 until his death. It has since
become the Ensor Museum. Photograph taken about
1898.
Das Haus, das Ensor von seinem Onkel mütter-
licherseits (Mann mit weißem Bart im Foto rechts)
erbte und von 1917 bis zu seinem Tode bewohnte.
Heute Ensor-Museum. Aufnahme um 1898.
La casa che Ensor ereditò dallo zio materno (a
destra nella fotografia, con la barba bianca) e che
abitò dal 1917 fino alla sua morte. Oggi Museo
Ensor. Fotografia del 1898 circa.

5

6

7

345

1 *Ensor on the Belgian coast (August 1932).*
From left to right: Albert Einstein; Marcel
Abraham, writer; Anatole de Monzie, French
Minister of Public Instruction; Ensor.
Begegnung an der belgischen Küste (August
1932). Von links nach rechts: Albert Ein-
stein; der Schriftsteller Marcel Abraham;
der französische Erziehungsminister Anatole
de Monzie; Ensor.
Incontro sulla costa belga (agosto 1932). Da
sinistra a destra: Albert Einstein; lo scrittore
Marcel Abraham; il ministro dell'educazione
francese Anatole de Monzie; Ensor.

2 *Ensor's studio (1921). Photograph of the*
ornamental silvered ball that hung from the
chandelier in the studio. Left: the painter
Constant Permeke, who lived in Ostend from
1892 to 1928; right: Ensor.
Ensors Atelier (1921). Aufnahme einer
versilberten Zierkugel des Leuchters im Ate-
lier. Links: der Maler Constant Permeke,
der von 1892 bis 1928 in Ostende lebte;
rechts: Ensor.
Lo studio di Ensor (1921). Fotografia di
una palla argentata appesa alla lampada
dello studio. A sinistra: il pittore Constant
Permeke, che visse a Ostenda dal 1892 al
1928; a destra: Ensor.

3 *Shipping "The Entry of Christ into*
Brussels". The painting was going to Paris, to
be shown at the Ensor exhibition organized by
the "Gazette des Beaux-Arts" in 1939.
Transport des »Einzug Christi in Brüssel«.
Das Bild ging nach Paris zu der Ensor-Aus-
stellung, die 1939 von der »Gazette des
Beaux-Arts« veranstaltet wurde.
Il trasporto dell' «Ingresso di Christo a
Bruxelles». L'opera andava a Parigi alla
mostra di Ensor organizzata dalla «Gazette
des Beaux Arts» nel 1939.

4 *Ensor and his manservant Auguste.*
Ensor und sein Diener Auguste.
Ensor e il suo domestico Auguste.

6 *Augusta Boogaerts, before the self-portrait*
of Ensor entitled "Portrait of the Painter in
a Flowered Hat" (1949)
Augusta Boogaerts vor dem Bild »Ensor mit
dem Blumenhut« (1949)
Augusta Boogaerts davanti al quadro «Ensor
col cappello infiorato» (1949)

5

5 Double Portrait – Doppelportrait – Doppio ritratto (1905)
Augusta Boogaerts, Ensor's great friend and reflected in a mirror, Ensor himself.
Augusta Boogaerts, Ensors Freundin, und im Spiegel sichtbar Ensor selber.
Augusta Boogaerts, l'amica di Ensor e riflesso nello specchio, James Ensor.

6

1—2 *Fun on the Dunes (1892). The poses of the two com-*
batants, the younger Ernest Rousseau and Ensor, reproduce
those of the "Skeletons Fighting for the Body of a Hanged
Man", which Ensor had painted a short time before (see p. 175,
c. c. 130).
Maskerade in den Dünen (1892). Die Pose der beiden
Kampfhähne Ernest Rousseau jun. und Ensor gibt die der
»Masken im Streit um einen Gehenkten« wieder, eines Bildes,
das Ensor kurz zuvor gemalt hatte (siehe S. 175, K. 130).
Scherzi fra la dune (1892). L'atteggiamento dei due contendenti,
Ernest Rousseau figlio e Ensor, ricorda quello delle «Maschere
che si contendono un impiccato», che Ensor aveva appena finito
di dipingere (v. p. 175, C. 130).

3 *Ensor playing the flute on the roof (c. 1885).*
Ensor bläst Flöte auf dem Dach (c. 1885).
Ensor suona il flauto sui tetti (c. 1885).

4 *Pyramid of Masks (c. 1890). Third from the bottom is*
Ensor.
Maskenpyramide (c. 1890). Der dritte von unten ist Ensor.
Piramide di maschere (c. 1890). Il terzo dal basso è Ensor.

5 *Ensor proclaimed Prince of Painters, Palace Hotel,*
Brussels (March 1933).
Ensor wird im Palace Hotel in Brüssel zum Malerfürsten
ausgerufen (März 1933).
Ensor viene proclamato Principe dei Pittori al Palace Hôtel di
Bruxelles (marzo 1933).

6 *Carnival at Ostend*
Karneval in Ostende
Carnevale a Ostenda

4

5

6

349

Ensor on the balcony of the former Ostend Casino (1921)
Ensor auf dem Balkon des ehemaligen Kursaals in Ostende (1921)
Ensor sul balcone del vecchio Kursaal di Ostenda (1921)

The beach at Ostend
Der Strand von Ostende
La spiaggia di Ostenda

Mantlepiece in Ensor's home
Kaminsims in Ensors Haus
Caminetto nella casa di Ensor

Photograph of the beach at Ostend
with a drawing by Ensor
Photographie des Ostender Strandes
mit einer Zeichnung Ensors
Cartolina illustrata della spiaggia di
Ostenda con un disegno di Ensor

Ensor in his studio
Ensor in seinem Atelier
Ensor nel suo studio

Ernst van Leiden. Portrait of James Ensor – Portrait James
Ensor – Ritratto di James Ensor (not dated – undatiert – senza
data)

Ensor playing the harmonium in his drawing-room studio (1937). In
front of him is "The Entry of Christ into Brussels".
Ensor in seinem Atelier am Harmonium (1937). Vor ihm der »Einzug Christi in Brüssel«.
Ensor suona l'harmonium nello studio (1937). Di fronte a lui «L'ingresso di Cristo a Bruxelles».

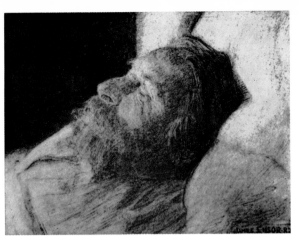

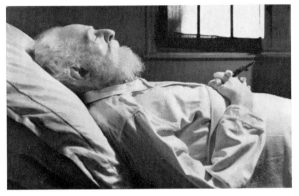

The Artist's Mother in Death – Ensors Mutter auf dem Totenbett – La madre di Ensor sul letto di morte (1915)

My Father on His Deathbed – Mein Vater auf dem Totenbett – Mio padre sul letto di morte (1887)

Ensor on his deathbed (November 1949)
Ensor auf dem Totenbett (November 1949)
Ensor sul letto di morte (novembre 1949)

Visiting card with ink drawing by Ensor
Visitenkarte mit Zeichnung Ensors
Biglietto da visita con un disegno di Ensor

ORIGINAL WRITINGS OF JAMES ENSOR*

THREE WEEKS AT THE ACADEMY
EPISODIC MONOLOGUE

The scene is the painting classroom.
Characters:

Three Teachers
The Head of the Academy
A Classroom Attendant
Silent Character: A future member of Les XX.

Note: The authenticity of the small talk that follows is guaranteed.

FIRST WEEK

*Professor Pielsticker:*** You are a colorist, Monsieur, but ninety painters out of a hundred are.
Your Flemishness is always coming out, no matter what you do. I find the French artists very good; at an exhibition you can tell them at once from their neighbors. They are very strong in composition. It's wrong to think that the teacher spoils a sketch when he corrects it. When I was your age I thought so too, but now I see that my teacher was right.
You're not making progress! This isn't rounded at all! (*Showing a sketch by another pupil*): Now, here's one who is going places! Unfortunately, he is too lazy.
You're already trying to render the atmosphere instead of waiting till your drawing is good enough. Remember, you still have two semesters of classical art! After that you'll have plenty of time for atmosphere, color, and the rest.
You don't want to learn! To paint like that is positively mad, wicked!
I *cannot help* complimenting you on your drawing; but why do you have to make drawings against the Academy?

---

* Ensor's writings, in eccentric French and filled with puns, pose many problems for the translator. He has, therefore, taken certain liberties in order to avoid the need for explanatory footnotes, even creating puns of his own in order to convey the spirit rather than the letter of Ensor's writings.

** The Dutch names of the teachers are fictitious, and are meant to be comical.

SECOND WEEK

Professor Slimmervogel: You've done your background instead of the figure; it's not difficult to do a background.

You do the opposite of what you're told. Instead of beginning with your strong accents, you begin with the light ones. How can you judge the whole? You must do your strong accents with black vine and burnt Sienna.

There's something funny going on here; never before have I seen a painting class like the one this year. I'd be ashamed if a stranger came in.

I don't see anything in this. There is color, but that's not enough. It lacks strength. You're putting the paint on too thick. You seem to be looking for something all right. But you've looked enough now.

Was it Mr. Pielsticker who corrected your sketch? But it isn't his week. How annoying!

THIRD WEEK

Professor Van Mollekot: What's that? It's much too brown, you know! Was it Slimmervogel who corrected you?

You started out so well. Your drawing is so good. But you ruin everything you do.

Believe me, I'm telling you this for your own good. Put your sketch next to the model. You're afraid to paint.

You must paint with flat brushes, lay it on thick, but you mustn't keep working it over. You're not putting it on thick enough. I know you know how to do it, but you have to show it to other people. You're doing a landscape? You're wasting your time on landscape!

The Head: But you're making your drawing as you go along! Bad! Bad! You're going to drown in all that paint.

It's feeling that ruins you, and you're not the only one.

Last week you made a good drawing, but now it's the same thing all over again. Do you have trouble with your eyes by any chance? A sculptor would be quite at a loss if he had to make something from your drawing.

Was it Mr. Slimmervogel who retouched this?

The Classroom Attendant: Mr. Pielsticker and the Head are very angry at you for what you submitted in the painting competition. If you'll promise me that you'll do another subject, I'll speak to the Head, and you can join the nature class.

Moral: The pupil quits the Academy and becomes a *vingtiste*.
Further moral: The Salon rejects his paintings.   1884

SPEECH AT THE ENSOR EXHIBITION AT THE JEU DU PAUME

Ladies, Young Ladies,

Gentlemen,

My dear Friends,

One sunny day my late friend François Franck of Antwerp came to see me and said, "Paris is the place one has to go, to be baptized and confirmed. Get into the dance, then, uphold your colors, those of our country, they will be fashionable." I have heeded his advice with joy and confidence. My dear friends of Paris.

I love three cities in Belgium – Antwerp, a vast crossroads of spring tides and puffy-faced virgins framed in painted paper; Liége, city of burning mines and mineral waters and black milk; and Ostend, related to Antwerp only by latitude, is mirrored in the opal.

The Flemish sea gives me all its nacreous fires, and I embrace it every morning, noon, and night. Ah, the wonderful kisses of my beloved sea, sublimated kisses, sandy, perfumed with foam, refreshingly pungent.

I salute you, Paris, and all your hills where people work and have fun. Paris, powerful magnet, all the big stars of Belgium cling to your sides. Paris, fetish, I have brought you my own little star, show me your best profile.

Dear friends, I recall 1929, the year of my most retrospective show at the Palais des Beaux-Arts in Brussels. Your generous critics vied with each other showering me with praise, and now your great men are interested in my labors.

Dear brothers-in-law of France, you will see close-up some of my interiors, my kitchen with curly cabbages, my barbate and striped fishes, my modern animalized goddesses, my lady friends with pursed lips rouged with adorable affection, my rebellious angels glimpsed in the clouds, and I will be well represented.

All my paintings have come I don't know where from, mostly from the sea.

And my suffering, scandalized, insolent, cruel, malicious masks, and a long time ago I could say and write, "trailed by followers I have joyfully shut myself in the solitary milieu ruled by the mask with a face of violence and brilliance."

And the mask cried to me: Freshness of tone, sharp expression, sumptuous decor, great unexpected gestures, unplanned movements, exquisite turbulence.

O the animal masks of the Ostend Carnival: bloated vicuna faces, misshapen birds with the tails of birds of paradise, cranes with sky-blue bills gabbling nonsense, clay-footed architects, obtuse sciolists with moldy skulls, heartless vivisectionists, odd insects, hard shells giving shelter to soft beasts.

Witness *The Entry of Christ into Brussels* which teems with all the hard and soft creatures spewed out by the sea. Won over by irony, touched by splendors, my vision becomes more refined, I purify my colors, they are whole and personal.

I see no heavy ochers in our country. Sterile ochers come from the earth, they shall return to the earth without drums or trumpets.

Ah, the tender flowers of painting were submerged by a wave of mud.

Tarnished, rancid, crackled under the smoky varnishes, or excessively washed and scrubbed, embellished and retouched, the masterpieces of the great old painters have nothing valuable to say. Iris is no longer there. Restorers, varnishers, listen to my ever-young motto:

Frogs that croak the loudest come closest to bursting.

Let us brighten our colors that they may sing, laugh, shout all their joys.

From the heights of the sacred hills of Paris, all lighthouses lit up, shine, green lights of youth, golds and silvers of maturity, pinks of maidenhood.

Roar Fauves, wild beasts, Dodos, Dadas, dance Expressionists, Futurists, Cubists, Surrealists, Orphists. Yours is a great art. Paris is great.

Let us encourage the painter's art and its diverse canons. Fire salvos upon salvos, cannoneers of art, for the salvation of color.

Color, color, life of things living and inanimate, enchantment of painting.

Colors of our dreams, colors of our loved ones.

Cannoneers, to your guns, and you too, lady-cannoneers. Fire your salvos to glorify the genius of your artists, fire blanks at painters too fond of comforts.

Painters and lady painters, my friends, your holy canons do not spew death but light and life.

Art of the celestial Empire, canon; Egyptian art, canon; Greek art, canon; Byzantine art, canon; Persian art, canon; Gothic art, canon; Academic, canon, canon; Classical, Romantic, canon; Realist, Impressionist, canon; Futurist, canon; Cubist, another canon; Expressionist, Negro, Dada, canon; Surrealist, art of the *douaniers*, again canon, canon, canon, indeed art imposes itself by means of cannon, religious art most of all.

Fine painters of France, the fresh choir of the Muses accompanies you. Yes, you create durable styles, impressive styles. Yes, your painting is amplified by seduction and new smiles.

I recall two great Antwerp painters, infatuated with fine subjects. The admirable Henri de Braekeleer, a magnificent, precious, meticulous painter till the day he died, and Jan Stobbaerts, colorist with rainy eyes full of motes and beams, this honest painter painted milch cows and milkmaids and one-headed calves.

Dear friends of Paris, you have praised me, comforted me, I thank you, and charmed, I answer: Paris the admirable, Paris the refuge of our fine painters, of our greatest poets, in short of our big and little Belgians, Paris the imperishable, the unique, the indivisible, Paris Queen of Art, Paris and the countryside around her.

I thank the organizers of the Salon du Jeu de Paume, the distinguished curator, and all our patrons, as well as my devoted friends of L'Art Contemporain of Antwerp and the indulgent collectors and all my defenders.

And a tribute in memory of François Franck, the friend with a heart of gold, the inspirer of the patrons of Antwerp and of Belgium.

I thank you, great Paris, first wonder of the world.

Paris, June 1932

TO EINSTEIN

Among ourselves I am taking the liberty of saluting a table companion of great weight, heavyweight or lightweight, a neighbor nimbused in importance, a block of science covered with flowers by a coastal colleague perched on a dune. Honor to you, great thinker, great launcher of probing rays, your face crowned with silver emanates millenary lights.

Yes, celestial bodies irradiate the paradise of Rotarian relativities, light up the closed field of our table where glasses, cups, crystals, flagons reflect the twinkles and silken and joyful cries of young stars on a spree, where firecrackers, candles, and rockets set fire to our senses and burn the mind with our thoughts.

But you, man of light, you reflect suns, take the inventory of planets, invent moons, invite comets, illustrate stars. What's more, and more useful, you extinguish lazy stars, you check brilliant meteors gone astray, eager to fall and to fall again.

Ladies, Gentlemen, forgive me for speaking so frivolously, forgive my humbly pictorial language, my words that are out of place, shrill or ambiguous, anti-mathematical, I have always condemned the worlds in which one is bored, and their plurality.

Our Rotarian brothers of China and America belch when they smoke; in our country, we dream when we eat, we think when we drink.

Here, dear friends, let us drink and fraternize under the sun veiled by the gray of the uncertain times. Alas! Three times alas!!! Painters slaves to vision remain rebellious to positive rays as well as to positive reason, to calculations, to probabilities; between reason and comprehension, between appearance and reality, the disagreement remains profound.

Now you will tell me, eminent scientist, that 6 is not 9. I shall answer you: All I have to do to get 9 out of 6 is to kick it over. And if you tell me that 6 and 8 is 14, I shall reply that 6 and 8 is 68. In such cases, Ladies, Gentlemen, everything is relative.

And it has always been said that there are more relative than absolute truths.

Let us know how to appreciate the old Belgo-opportunistic slogan: Light bursts forth from the clash of ideas.

Dear master, accept my tribute. Excuse my words peppered with feeling. My thanks to you, friends, come from the heart and from the hand in the curving line of life and merriment.

Come from the heart, the great incandescent focal point, from the heart which sometimes strikes twelve at 2:00 p. m., but which is nonetheless a masterpiece of the divine clockmaker.

Let us roundly praise the great Einstein and his relative orders, but let us condemn the algebrist with his square roots, the landsurveyor with his cubic reason.

I say the world is round, as well as the divine sun and my lady the moon, round are the cheeks, round are the dimples, round the pupils, round the apples, round the plates, round the rumps, round the cups, but let us sing squarely this time, Ladies, Gentlemen, and in chorus, please: "There is only one Einstein who rules in the heavens."

Ostend, August 1933

ON WOMEN - 1925

Deceiving sex, respector neither of law nor of religion, heartless and devoid of honor
Sink of hypocrisy
Hotbed of lies and dissimulation
Mud-pit of malice
Cavern of greed and the deadly sins
Pandora box
Miry pool crawling with bad beasts
Liquid manure, sticky and oozing with vermin
Sneaky and hostile morass
Horrible cesspool teeming with leeches
Beast with claws and suckers and teeth for tearing live flesh
Blowing she-satyr, blowing hot and cold
Inspirer of the worst villainies
Treacherous in friendship
Gamy hen, proud and stupid
Featherbrained goose
Unscrupulous climber looking for accomplices
Weather vane creaking with every ill wind
Triple hole of felony, unfathomable betrayal, and devouring selfishness
Vast walking lie, belly forward, bottom tastefully larded
The scourge of heaven and of earth
Constant mask and endless smile.

(By courtesy of Henri Storck, who owns the original.)

To praise my friends and to understand them better
A long line
A short line
And the iridescent color of the sea
A tribute to those faithful yesterday
Today and always

Ostend, October 10, 1945

BEAUTY IN DANGER: THE DUNES

Protest! The virginity of the dunes is threatened from Ostend to Blankenberghe. Keep after the inexcusable desecrators, harass the conceited asses, dreary imbeciles, limping architects, clumsy fools, preposterous and impudent bunglers, wreckers of scenery, spiteful dune-ophobes, brazen thistle-philes.

Cry over the polluted breast-shaped hills, the rounded rumps, the nests of yellow woods, the tubercular vegetables, the prosaic cabbages.

Why ransack, ravage, mess up, murder, fence off, trim, cut, mask, smoke, tame, spoil, deflower, level, polish, befoul, bestink adorable sites worthy of respect?

Take your example from England, you barbarian architects, you frenzied woodchoppers, you wreckers respecting neither law nor religion.

Alas! The Belgians are devoid of feeling. They destroy landscapes, torture plants, torment animals, break young trees, they are out-and-out vandals.

Kingdom of sullen bores and civil engineers, Belgium has lost its beauties, irretrievably.

I appeal to artists, the only competent judges.

Protest! Protest! Protest!

A CHRONOLOGY OF THE PRINCIPAL EVENTS OF ENSOR'S LIFE

1860   James Sidney Ensor is born in Ostend, Belgium, at No. 44 Rue Longue, on Friday, April 13. As he later remembered it, the house was set in large gardens and looked down over the verdant walls of the old city. Since then it has been altered in appearance, and today bears the number 26. James's father, Frederic-James Ensor, born in Brussels on October 27, 1833, was of British extraction. His mother, Maria-Catharina Haegheman (called Catherine), had also been born in Ostend (on April 24, 1835), and was of old Flemish stock. Ostend, the largest town on the Belgian coast (population 16,000 in 1860, today 54,000) is well known as a seaside resort and spa. During the summer season it is much frequented by Belgians from all over the country, and by an ever-increasing number of vacationists from the rest of Europe. James's parents, like certain other members of the family, made their living selling "souvenirs of Ostend" – beach toys, knickknacks, seashells, curios, imported objects, and, during the Carnival season, masks. There was always such a shop on the ground floor of the various houses Ensor lived in, and the objects sold there, with which he was familiar from his childhood, were one of the major sources of his inspiration.

1861   On August 29, Mariette Ensor (nicknamed "Mitche"), James's only sister (he had no brothers) is born in Ostend. As a young girl she frequently poses as a model for Ensor.

1873   Age 13. James enters the Collège Notre-Dame at Ostend. He remains there for only two years: he is a poor student. His schoolmates are struck by his inability to comply with the regulations. He begins to draw in black-and-white and in color. Aware of his talent his parents arrange for lessons with two Ostend watercolorists, Dubar and Van Kuyck, whose works have not survived.

1875   Age 15. James's parents who had moved with their shop from the Rue Longue, first to a house at the corner of Rue d'Ouest and Rue Christine, and then to No. 66 (now 44) of the Rue Longue, finally move to the house at the corner of the Rue de Flandre and the Boulevard Van Iseghem. James Ensor will live there until 1917.

1876   Age 16. Ensor executes his first paintings, small works on cardboard, painted out-of-doors and representing the dunes, the sea, and the countryside.

1877   Age 17. James enters the Brussels Academy directed by Jean Portaels. The teachers include Alexandre Robert, Joseph Stallaert, and Jef Van Severdonck. Among Ensor's classmates, with whom he becomes intimate, are Crespin, Charlet, Duyck, and Fernand Khnopff. – He paints a remarkable academic study, entitled *The Model*. – While in Brussels, Ensor lives in a modest room in the Rue Saint-Jean.

1878   Age 18. Year is spent at the Academy. Ensor paints several compositions which never get beyond the stage of preliminary studies: *Judith and Holofernes*, *Death of Jezebel*, etc.

1879   Age 19. Year is spent at the Brussels Academy. – Main works: *Girl With the Turned-Up Nose*, and three small self-portraits, which are already major works, filled with the authentic spirit of Ensor's first period. They inaugurate the so-called "somber" period which extends until about 1883. However, during this year Ensor paints his first mask picture: *Mask Gazing at a Negro Mountebank.* – He begins to frequent the circle around Professor Ernest Rousseau, where he will make friendships, and which will exert a great influence on his ideas as well as on his art.

1880 Age 20. James leaves the Brussels Academy and settles in Ostend. He occupies a studio in the attic of his parents' home, from which he can look out over the streets and rooftops of the town, to the sea and to the surrounding countryside. He will execute his main works in this garret studio. Major works of this year: *Mystic Death of a Theologian* (drawing), *The Lamp Boy*, *Lady with a Fan, The Colorist, Still Life with Duck*, as well as an important series of charcoal drawings of ordinary local types. Ensor keeps in touch with Brussels, where he often visits the Rousseaus in their house at No. 20 Rue Vautier. Thus he escapes from the sometimes stifling Ostend atmosphere. The Rousseaus provide him with sympathy and understanding. In their home in Brussels, a meeting place for bold and original minds, he finds a congenial "milieu."

1881 Age 21. For the first time Ensor takes part in an exhibition, organized by La Chrysalide, a group which includes Dubois, Artan, Vogels, Rops, Pantazis, and others. It is held in the Janssens hall, part of a rug store owned by Eugène Demolder's father in the Rue du Petit Ecuyer (today Rue du Gentilhomme) in Brussels. The press reviews are at first favorable, but the tone soon changes, and as time goes on the hostility will mount. – Ensor is in full possession of his powers: he paints the *Portrait of the Artist's Father, Russian Music, Afternoon at Ostend, The Bourgeois Salon, Somber Lady, Lady in Blue, Rue de Flandre in the Sun.*

1882 Age 22. Principal works: *The Painter Willy Finch, Sick Tramp Warming Himself* (destroyed during the bombardment of Ostend during World War II), *Woman Eating Oysters, Waiting, Troubled (La Dame en détresse).* – *Woman Eating Oysters* is rejected by the Antwerp Salon. Ensor and Vogels are exhibited at the Cercle Artistique of Brussels. Ensor's works are branded as "turpitudes," and a petition demanding that they be withdrawn from the exhibition is circulated among the members of the Cercle.

1883 Age 23. Exhibition with the *avant-garde* group L'Essor, which accepts *The Lamp Boy*, but rejects *Woman Eating Oysters.* Principal works: *The Rower, The Drunkards, Scandalized Masks, Portrait of the Painter in a Flowered Hat.* – Octave Maus founds the group Les XX (The Twenty) which exists until 1893. Ensor is one of the members; the others are Chainaye, Charlet, Delvin, Dubois, Finch, Goethals, Khnopff, Lambeaux, Pantazis, Dario de Regoyas, Schlobach, Simons, Vanaise, Van Rysselberghe, Van Strijdonck, Verhaert, Verstraete, Vogels, and Wytsman. The group also played avant-garde music, sponsored lectures by *auteurs maudits*, and invited the boldest foreign painters to exhibit with them. Ensor took part fairly regularly in the annual exhibitions of Les XX, which shocked the public and precipitated a real battle for artistic freedom. However, on several occasions Maus and other members of Les XX asked Ensor to withdraw certain works he had submitted, on the ground that they were indefensibly, pointlessly shocking.

1884 Age 24. The Brussels Salon rejects all the works Ensor submits, including *Afternoon at Ostend*. – Principal works: *Ostend Rooftops*, *The White Cloud*, *Interior* (representing the Rousseaus' home in Brussels). Ensor's first written work, "Three Weeks at the Academy" is published in *L'Art Moderne*: it is an impertinent parody of the teaching at the Brussels Academy (p. 355). He later published occasional essays on art, reviews, and letters of protest (against vivisection, against the destruction of dunes and old docks in Ostend). These pieces appeared in various periodicals – *L'Art Moderne*, *La Ligue Artistique*, *La Plume*, *Le Coq Rouge*, *Pourquoi Pas?*, *La Saison à Ostende* – and their irreverent tone earned for their author some lasting enmities.

1885 Age 25. Principal works: *Haunted Furniture* (destroyed during World War II), *Skeletons Looking at "Chinoiseries,"* *Lighthouse at Ostend*, *Hôtel de Ville, Brussels*, and a large drawing, *Hail Jesus, King of the Jews*, the composition and general spirit of which foreshadow *The Entry of Christ into Brussels*. – The hostility of the official critics is now almost unanimous.

1886 Age 26. Principal oils: *Children Dressing*, *Descent from the Cross*. First etchings, among them, *Christ Mocked*, *Christ Calming the Waters*, and *The Cathedral*. In the next thirteen years Ensor will execute the 115 plates that comprise the major portion of his work as an engraver. – Isidore Verheyden paints a portrait of Ensor in a derby hat and a putty-colored overcoat.

1887 Age 27. Ensor's father dies in Ostend, at the age of 52. James executes a series of drawings of his father on his deathbed. – Principal works: *Carnival on the Beach*, *Adam and Eve Driven From Paradise*, *The Tribulations of Saint Anthony*. Although Ensor may use various manners in a single painting, and although the paintings he sends to a single exhibit may be in various styles, his "somber" period may be regarded as having come to an end during the years 1884–86, and he is now fully entered in his "light" period. For the entirety of his long career, he will never again return to the subdued tones of his "somber" period. However, in referring to the "light" period, we usually designate a period of only twelve years (1887–1900) during which his activity will be particularly intense and inventive. According to Demolder, a drawing depicting *Christ's entry into Jerusalem*, caused a row at the exhibition of Les XX: this drawing may have been *Hail Jesus, King of the Jews*, executed in 1885.

1888 Age 28. Les XX rejects works submitted by Ensor, including *Children Dressing* and *The Tribulations of Saint Anthony*. Principal works: *The Entry of Christ Into Brussels Masks Confronting Death*, *Garden of Love*. – While Ensor continues to be reviled by most of of the critics, a number of the younger writers – Verhaeren, Picard, Maeterlinck, Eekhoud, and particularly Eugène Demolder – offer him their friendship and support. Augusta Boogaerts (1870–1950), daughter of an Ostend hotel owner, becomes Ensor's friend and companion. He calls her "La Sirène." Though they see each other only intermittently, their union lasts to the end of their lives.

1889 Age 29. Principal works: *The Fall of the Rebellious Angels*, *Skeletons Trying to Warm Themselves*, *Old Woman with Masks*, *Astonishment of the Mask Wouse*, *Attributes of the Studio*. The works he submits for exhibition at Les XX, including the *Entry of Christ into Brussels*, are refused. A proposal to expel him from the group is defeated by one vote, his own. His desire to remain affiliated was dictated by the fact that only at Les XX did he have a chance to exhibit. – *After-*

noon at Ostend, hangs for several years at the Ostend Casino with a for-sale sign. Though the price is only 350 francs, it finds no buyer.

1890 Age 30. Principal works: *Intrigue, Murder, The Embroiderer, Ensor and General Leman Discussing Painting, The Artist at the Easel.* – Les XX rejects a number of Ensor's entries, including *Masks Confronting Death* and *Astonishment of the Mask Wouse.*

1891 Age 31. Principal works: *Skeletons Fighting for the Body of a Hanged Man, The Tragic Musicians, The Judges, Ecce Homo, Music, Rue de Flandre, Skeletons Disputing a Herring.*

1892 Age 32. Principal works: *The Despair of Pierrot, Melancholy Fishwives, The Skate, The Cabbage, Boats on the Beach* (first version), *My Favorite Room, Consoling Virgin.* – Ensor visits London for a few days. – Demolder writes the first study praising him. – Mitche Ensor marries a Chinese, Tan Hee Tseu, who leaves her shortly after the wedding, but by whom she has a daughter, Alexandra, the future Madame Daveluy. Mitche and her daughter live with Ensor.

1893 Age 33. Principal works: *Pierrot and Skeleton, The Boulevard Van Iseghem, Portrait of Eugène Demolder.* – Misunderstood by those around him, and exasperated by his failure, Ensor offers to sell everything in his studio for 8,500 francs. Despite his efforts and those of some of his friends, the hoped-for sale does not take place. – Octave Maus dissolves Les XX and replaces it by La Libre Esthétique (1894–1914), a new group under his leadership, which excludes the artists of the former group.

1894 Age 34. Principal works: *Combat* and *The Temptation of Saint Anthony.*

1895 Age 35. Principal works: *Seashells, Fish, Flowers and Masks, Still Life with Rooster.*

1896 Age 36. Principal works: *Dangerous Cooks, Flowers and Chinese Vase, Flowers and Vegetables.* – Demolder organizes the first Ensor exhibition in the Rue Montagne-aux-Herbes-Potagères in Brussels. – *The Lamp Boy* (painted fifteen years earlier) is purchased by the Brussels Museum.

1897 Age 37. Principal work: *Masks and Death.*

1898 Age 38. Small Ensor exhibition is organized by the review *La Plume* in Paris, at No. 31 Rue Bonaparte. It passes unnoticed.

1899 Age 39. Principal work: *Portrait of the Artist Surrounded by Masks.* – Eugène Demolder induces the Paris review *La Plume* to devote a special issue to Ensor. Unnoticed at the time of publication, in years to come this issue will be at a premium.

1900 Age 40. Principal works: *Skeletons in the Studio* and *Boats on the Beach* (second version). About this time (or even four or five years earlier) Ensor's production begins to slow down. The reasons for this are obscure. He will execute important works in the years ahead, but his creative powers seem to decline, and his technique and inspiration weaken.

1901 Age 41. Principal work: *Kermess With Blood Sausages.* – Edmond Picard creates *La Libre Académie de Belgique.* Ensor is brought into it as one of the founders.

1903 Age 43. Ensor is named a Knight of the Order of Leopold. – Emma Lambotte visits Ensor, who calls her "Emaël." She buys some of his works, and publishes essays on him.

1904 Age 44. Principal works: *Virgin with Masked Donors*; series of etchings including *Peste dessus, peste dessous, peste partout* and *The Seven Deadly Sins.*

1905 Age 45. Principal work: *Double Portrait*, representing Ensor and Augusta Boogaerts. – The Ensors engage the services of Auguste Van Yper (called Gust) and Ernestine Mollet. Ensor later has them live with him as his personal servants. – An Antwerp patron of the arts, François Franck, becomes a champion of Ensor's art. A leading member of *L'Art Contemporain*, he induces this group to show important collections of his protégé's work at Antwerp. Later, thanks to his interest and generosity, many works by Ensor are introduced into the museums of that city.

1907 Age 47. Principal works: *Pierrot and Skeletons, Skeleton Musicians*. – Henri de Groux paints a portrait of Ensor, entitled *Ensor Surrounded by Masks*.

1908 Age 48. Emile Verhaeren's monograph on James Ensor is published in Brussels.

1911 Age 51. Ensor composes the score, writes the scenario, and designs the costumes and settings for his pantomime ballet *La Gamme d'Amour (Flirt de Marionettes)*. The German Expressionist painter Emil Nolde visits Ensor, and subsequently makes masks the principal theme of his works.

1912 Age 52. Principal works: Trial settings for the 1st and 2nd Acts of the ballet *La Gamme d'Amour*, and 36 colored drawings forming the series of *Scenes from the Life of Christ*.

1913 Age 53. Principal work: *War of the Snails* (drawing). Garvens-Garvensburg in Hanover publishes the first catalogue of Ensor's etchings. – Rik Wouters makes his bust of Ensor. – Death of Ensor's close friend, Eugène Demolder.

1915 Age 55. Death of Ensor's mother, Catherine Haegheman, at the age of 80. Ensor executes several paintings and drawings of his dead mother. He also paints a large decorative panel, *The Mask is Off*.

1916 Age 56. Death of Ensor's aunt, Marie-Louise Haegheman, whom he occasionally used as a model. Principal work: *The Catafalque (or Chère morte)*.

1917 Age 57. Ensor moves from the building on the corner of the Rue de Flandre and the Boulevard Van Iseghem to No. 17 Rue de Flandre (today No. 27), a modest private house he inherited from his uncle Leopold Haegheman. He keeps the ground-floor shop of toys, seashells, and souvenirs, but does not reopen it for business. In this house where he will stay until his death, he hospitably receives ever larger numbers of visitors, who come from everywhere to pay their homage to the master. A considerable number of his best canvases are hung in a studio-parlor on the second floor, which serves as a kind of private museum.

1920 Age 60. Principal work: *Christ Among the Doctors*. The Giroux gallery in Brussels organizes the first great retrospective exhibition of Ensor's works. His ballet *La Gamme d'Amour*, directed by Léon Delcroix, is performed at the gallery. – De Ridder and Van Hecke found the magazine Sélection (1920–30) which defends the Flemish Expressionists and hails Ensor as a Precursor.

1921 Age 61. Great new retrospective exhibition, this time at the Salon de l'Art Contemporain in Antwerp. – Editions Sélection in Brussels publishes *Les Ecrits d'Ensor*. – The Giroux gallery publishes *Scènes de la Vie du Christ*, from the colored drawings dating from 1912. – A monograph on Ensor by Paul Colin is published in Germany.

1922 Age 62. Principal work: *The Road to Calvary*. – Publication of Grégoire Le Roy's monograph on Ensor.

1925 Age 65. Principal work: *The Rape of Andromeda*. – Loys Delteil publishes the complete catalogue of Ensor's engravings.

1926 Age 66. Principal work: *La Ruée des Disciples du Christ.* – First important exhibition in Paris at the Galerie Barbazanges. – Ensor's works shown at the Belgian pavilion of the Venice Biennale.

1927 Age 67. Large Ensor exhibition in Hanover, at the Kestner Gesellschaft.

1929 Age 69. The inaugural exhibition at the Palais des Beaux-Arts in Brussels is devoted to Ensor. Almost all his works are assembled there. Ensor is made a Baron by King Albert.

1931 Age 71. Ensor attends the unveiling of his own monument, by the sculptor Edmond de Valeriola, which is set up near the Ostend Casino. – Flor Alpaerts' *Suite James Ensor* is performed in Antwerp.

1932 Age 72. Important Ensor exhibition at the Musée du Jeu de Paume in Paris. – François Franck, Ensor's patron and great champion, dies in Ostend.

1933 Age 73. Principal works: *Port of Ostend* and *Ensor at the Harmonium.* – At a celebration organized in Brussels in his honor, Ensor is proclaimed "Prince of Painters." – The French minister Anatole de Monzie brings him the Cravate de la Légion d'Honneur.

1938 Age 78. Founding of Les Compagnons de l'Art (1938–46) in which Ensor is the principal figure.

1939 Age 79. Ensor exhibition in Paris, organized by *La Gazette des Beaux-Arts.*

1943 Age 83. Publication of Paul Fierens' monograph on Ensor.

1945 Age 85. Ensor's sister dies at the age of 84.

1946 Age 86. Important retrospective exhibition entitled "The Works of James Ensor" at the National Gallery in London.

1948 Age 88. Under the patronage of Queen Elizabeth and on the initiative of Madame Léon Wielemans, president, A. Croquez, H. Serruys, and J. Stevo, the club Les Amis de James Ensor is founded. It sets itself the task of publicizing the works of Ensor and creating an Ensor Museum at Ostend.

1949 Age 89. After an illness of three weeks, Ensor dies in an Ostend clinic, at daybreak, on November 19. He is buried just outside the town, in the little cemetery of the church of Notre-Dame des Dunes at Mariakerke. Shortly before his death, an exhibition entitled "Les gloires de la peinture moderne" was organized at Ostend; around works by Ensor, such as *The Entry of Christ into Brussels*, were hung paintings by Matisse, Braque, Chagall, Picasso, Klee, Max Ernst, De Chirico, and Dali.

On each anniversary of Ensor's death, Les Amis de James Ensor gather at Ostend to pay tribute to the man whose memory they strive to keep alive. A national subscription organized by the same society provided funds to purchase the house where Ensor last lived. The municipality, in collaboration with Les Amis, transformed it into a museum, where numerous souvenirs of the painter and some of his works are assembled. In 1950, twenty-five of his major works were hung in the Belgian pavilion of the Venice Biennale. In 1951 the Antwerp Museum arranged a large retrospective show, assembling more than 400 paintings, drawings, and etchings. The same year, a selection of 130 works was exhibited in the United States in New York, Boston, Cleveland, and St. Louis.

BIBLIOGRAPHY

ENSOR'S LITERARY, GRAPHIC, AND MUSICAL WORK

Les Ecus. Ostend, 1904. With 14 drawings, some in color

"James Ensor par lui-même," in *Pourquoi Pas?* (Brussels), December 21, 1911

Scènes de la Vie du Christ. Brussels, 1921. With 32 lithographs in color

Les Ecrits de James Ensor. Brussels, 1921. With 35 drawings

La Gamme d'Amour. Brussels, 1929. With 22 plates in color

Les Ecrits de James Ensor (1928–1934). Antwerp, 1934

Les Ecrits de James Ensor. Brussels, 1944. With an introduction by Henri Vandeputte

GENERAL

Lemonnier, Camille. *Histoire des Beaux-Arts en Belgique.* Brussels, 1887

Du Jardin, Jules. *L'Art flamand.* Brussels, 1900

Pica, Vittorio. *Studienköpfe.* Berlin, 1902

Mont, Pol de. *Koppen en Busten.* Brussels, 1903

Muther, Richard. *Die belgische Malerei im neunzehnten Jahrhundert.* Berlin, 1904. Published also in French, Brussels, 1904

Lemonnier, Camille. *L'Ecole belge de peinture, 1830–1905.* Brussels, 1906

Croquez, Albert. *Peintres flamands d'aujourd'hui.* Brussels, 1910

Lambotte, Paul. *Les Peintres de Portraits.* Brussels, 1913

Coquiot, Gustave. *Cubistes, Futuristes et Passéistes.* Paris, 1914

Mont, Pol de. *De Schilderkunst in Belgie van 1830 tot 1921.* The Hague, 1921

Van Zype, Gustave. *L'Art belge du XIXe siècle.* Brussels, 1923

Fontaine, André. *L'Art belge.* Paris, 1925

Fels, Florent. *Propos d'Artistes.* Paris, 1925

Maus, Madeleine Octave. *Trente Années de lutte pour l'art.* Brussels, 1926

Pierard, Louis. *Peinture belge contemporaine.* Paris, 1928

Focillon, Henri. *La Peinture aux XIXe et XXe siècles*. Paris, 1928

Colin, Paul. *La Peinture belge depuis 1830*. Brussels, 1930

Haesaerts, Luc and Paul. *Flandre, L'Impressionisme*. Paris, 1931

Colin, Paul. "L'Impressionisme en Belgique," in René Huyghe (ed.), *Histoire de l'Art contemporain*. Paris, 1933–34. vol. II, pp. 275–83

Fierens, Paul. *L'Art en Belgique*. Brussels, 1938

Haesaerts, Luc. *Histoire du Portrait, de Navez à Ensor*. Brussels, 1942

Lhote, André. *Ecrits sur la peinture*. Paris, 1946

Sterling, Charles. *La Nature Morte de l'antiquité à nos jours*. Paris, 1952

Stubbe, Achilles. *De Vlaamse Schilderkunst van Van Eyck tot Permeke*. Brussels, 1953

Poirier, Pierre. *La Peinture belge d'autrefois, 1830–1930*. Brussels, 1953

Legrand, F. C. *La Peinture en Belgique des Primitifs à nos jours*. Brussels, 1954

Haftmann, Werner. *Malerei im 20. Jahrhundert*. 2 vols. Munich, 1954–55

Barr, Alfred H., Jr. (ed.). *Masters of Modern Art*. New York, 1954

Haesaerts, Paul. *Constantes de la Peinture en Belgique*. Brussels, 1955

Huyghe, René. *Dialogue avec le visible*. Paris, 1955

MONOGRAPHS

Demolder, Eugène. *James Ensor*. Brussels, 1892; Paris, 1899

Pica, Vittorio. *James Ensor*. Bergamo, 1902

Verhaeren, Emile. *James Ensor*. Brussels, 1908

Colin, Paul. *James Ensor*. Potsdam, 1921

Le Roy, Gregoire. *James Ensor*. Brussels and Paris, 1922

Cuypers, Firmin. *James Ensor, L'Homme et l'Oeuvre*. Paris, 1925

Desmeth, Paul. *James Ensor*. Brussels, 1926

Fierens, Paul. *James Ensor*. Paris, 1929

De Ridder, André. *James Ensor*. Paris, 1930

Colin, Paul. *James Ensor*. Berlin, 1931

Teugels, Jean. *Variations sur James Ensor*. Ostend, 1931

Schwob, Lucien. *Ensor*. Brussels, 1936

Desmeth, Paul. *Paysages bruxellois, suivis d'une étude sur James Ensor*. Rev. ed. Brussels, 1937

Puyvelde, Leo van. *L'Ardente peinture d'Ensor*. Paris, 1939

Muls, Jozef. *James Ensor, peintre de la mer*. (Musées royaux des beaux-arts de Belgique. Conférences. 1940–41). Brussels, 1941

Fierens, Paul. *James Ensor*. Paris, 1943

Payro, Julio E. *James Ensor*. Buenos Aires, 1943

Fierens, Paul. *Les dessins d'Ensor*. Brussels, 1944

Fels, Florent. *James Ensor*. Geneva, 1947

Avermaete, Roger. *James Ensor*. London, 1951

Stevo, Jean. *James Ensor*. Brussels, 1947

Fierens, Paul (and others). *James Ensor, le Maître et sa Maison*. Brussels, 1956

Edebau, Frank. *La maison de James Ensor*. Brussels, 1957

ARTICLES

Demolder, Eugène. "James Ensor," in *Revue des Beaux-Arts et des Lettres* (Brussels), 1892

Mont, Pol de. "De Schilder en Etser James Ensor," in *De Vlaamsche School* (Antwerp), 1895

Demolder, Eugène. "James Ensor," in *La Libre Critique* (Brussels), 1895

La Plume (Paris), 1898. Special issue devoted to Ensor; articles by Camille Lemonnier, Edmond Picard, Emile Verhaeren, Camille Mauclair, Octave Maus, Blanche Rousseau, Georges Lemmen, Maurice des Ombiaux, Christian Beck, Jules Du Jardin, Pol de Mont, Louis Delattre, Octave Uzanne. Also issued separately, Paris, 1899

Coquiot, Gustave. "James Ensor," in *La Vogue* (Paris), 1899

Mauclair, Camille. "Les Peintres Belges," in *La Revue Bleue* (Paris), 1905

Croquez, Albert. "James Ensor, peintre et graveur," in *La Flandre Artiste* (Courtrai), 1908

Croquez, Albert. "James Ensor, peintre et graveur," in *La Fédération artistique* (Brussels), 1909

Brunt, Ary. "James Ensor," in *Onze Kunst* (Antwerp), 1911

Brunt, Ary. "James Ensor," in *Art flamand et hollandais* (Antwerp), 1911

Delen, A. J. J. "James Ensor," in *Elsevier's Geïllustreerd Maandschrift* (Amsterdam), 1911

Buschman, P. "Ensor," in U. Thieme and F. Becker, *Allgemeines Lexikon der bildenden Künstler*. Leipzig, 1914. vol. X, p. 569

Hausenstein, W. "James Ensor," in *Das Kunstblatt* (Weimar), 1918

Colin, Paul. "James Ensor," in *L'Amour de l'Art* (Paris), 1921

Fierens, Paul. "L'Art belge depuis l'impressionisme," in *L'Amour de l'Art* (Paris), September 1922

Fierens, Paul. "La Peinture et la Sculpture belges d'aujourd'hui," in *L'Amour de l'Art* (Paris), April 1923

La Flandre Littéraire (Ghent), 1924. Special issue devoted to James Ensor; articles by Edmond Picard, Georges Eekhoud, Hubert Krains, Fierens-Gevaert, Georges Virrès, Edmond Joly, Henri Vandeputte, Claude Bernières, Georges Ramaekers, A. J. J. Delen, André De Ridder, Franz Hellens, Gaston Heux, and Daan Boens

Hellens, Franz. "James Ensor," in *Nieuwe Kunst* (Amsterdam), 1924

Kremlicka. "Ensors Kindheit," in *Das Kunstblatt* (Weimar), 1924

Smet, Frédéric de. "James Ensor," in *Gand Artistique* (Ghent), 1925

Fierens, Paul. "Die junge Kunst in Belgien," in *Der Cicerone* (Leipzig), April 1925

Hellens, Franz. "Un grand peintre belge: James Ensor," in *L'Art Vivant* (Paris), January 1926

Hellens, Franz. "Nos Peintres: James Ensor," in *La Revue belge* (Brussels), 1926

Jaloux, Edmond. "James Ensor," in *L'Amour de l'Art* (Paris), May 1926

Habicht, V. C. "James Ensor," in *Deutsche Kunst und Dekoration* (Darmstadt), 1927

Woestijne, Karel van de. "James Ensor: Aspecten," in *Elsevier's Geïllustreerd Maandschrift* (Amsterdam), February 1928

De Ridder, André. "James Ensor à Ostende," in *Variétés* (Brussels), June 1928

Marlier, Georges. "James Ensor et le double aspect de son art," in *L'Amour de l'Art* (Paris), November 1928

Cahiers de Belgique (Brussels), 1929. Special issue devoted to James Ensor; articles by Paul Fierens, A. H. Cornette, and J. E. Sonderregger

Bernard, Charles. "James Ensor," in *La Revue d'Art* (Antwerp), January 1929

De Ridder, André. "James Ensor," in *Le Centaure* (Brussels), April 1929

Chabot, G. "Pour l'Art d'Ensor," in *Gand Artistique* (Ghent), 1929

Fierens, Paul. "Ensor et les Dunes," in *Variétés* (Brussels), October 1929

Carter, Frederick. "James Ensor," in *Artwork* (London), 1931

Linfest, Carl. "James Ensor," in *Belvedere* (Vienna), 1931

Alexandre, Arsène. "James Ensor à Paris," in *La Renaissance* (Paris), 1932

Marlier, Georges. "Exposition de James Ensor au Musée du Jeu de Paume," in *Formes* (Paris), 1932

Cornette, A. H. "James Ensor," in *La Revue d'Art* (Antwerp), 1932

Benson, E. M. "James Ensor," in *Parnassus* (New York), 1934

Muls, Jozef. "James Ensor, peintre de la mer," in *IIe Congrès international de la mer* (Liége), 1939

Fierens, Paul. "Visite à James Ensor," in *Documents* (Brussels), April 1940

Tannenbaum, Libby. "James Ensor: Prophet of Modern Fantastic Art," in *Magazine of Art* (Washington, D. C.), November 1943

Jedlicka, Gotthard. "James Ensor," in *Werk* (Zurich), 1944

Haesaerts, Paul. "L'apport belge à la Peinture contemporaine," in *Arts de France* (Paris), 1946

Croquez, Albert. "La jeunesse de James Ensor," in *L'Amour de l'Art* (Paris), 1947

Haesaerts, Paul. "Ensor," in *Les Peintres célèbres* (Geneva-Paris), 1948

Arts (Paris), November 24, 1949. Article by Paul Fierens, Paul Haesaerts, and R. L. Delevoy

"Hommage à James Ensor," in *Les Arts Plastiques* (Brussels), February 1950. Articles by Paul Fierens, René Huyghe, Jean Cassou, Paul Haesaerts, Louis Lebeer, and Jean Stevo

De Maeyer, Charles. "Ensor," in *Dictionnaire des peintres*. Brussels, 1950

Podesta, Attilio. "James Ensor," in *Emporium* (Bergamo), 1950

Hoffmann, Edith. "James Ensor," in *Burlington Magazine* (London), 1950

Les Beaux-Arts (Brussels), November 16, 1950. Articles by L. L. Sosset and André Souris

Haesaerts, Paul. "L'Expressionisme dans la Peinture européenne d'aujourd'hui," in *Reflets du Monde* (Brussels), March 1952

De Vlieger, Joseph M. "L'Entrée du Christ à Bruxelles ou Ensor à 1888," in *Reflets du Tourisme* (Brussels), December 1953

Haesaerts, Paul. "Ensor," in *Plaisir de France*, No. 187 bis (Paris), 1954

Fels, Florent. "Ensor à Paris," in *Les Nouvelles Littéraires* (Paris), February 25, 1954

Marx, Claude-Roger. "Du carnaval à l'au-delà en compagnie de James Ensor," in *Le Figaro Littéraire* (Paris), February 27, 1954

Elgar, Frank. "Ensor," in Fernand Hazan (ed.), *Dictionary of Modern Painting*. New York, 1956

Rosman, Corrie. "Ensor démasqué?" in *Nieuw Vlaams Tijdschrift* (Antwerp), 1957

EXHIBITION CATALOGUES

1920. Brussels. Galerie Georges Giroux. Commentary by J. F. Elslander

1926. Paris. Galerie Barbazanges. Introduction by Waldemar George

1927. Hanover. Kestner-Gesellschaft. *James Ensor: Festschrift zur ersten deutschen Ensor-Ausstellung.* Articles by A. Dörner, H. von Garvens-Garvensburg, and W. Fraenger

1929. Brussels. Palais des Beaux-Arts. Preface by François Fosca [pseudonym of Georges de Traz]

1932. Paris, Musée National du Jeu de Paume. Introduction by A. H. Cornette

1934. Stockholm. Liljevalcks Konsthall. Preface by Willy Konninck

1936. London. Leicester Galleries. Foreword by R. H. Wilensky. Reviewed in *Apollo* (London) 1936

1939. Paris. Galerie de la Gazette des Beaux-Arts. Introduction by Leo Van Puyvelde

1944. New York. Buchholz Gallery. Introduction by Leo Van Puyvelde

1945. Brussels. Galerie Georges Giroux. Introduction by Leo Van Puyvelde

1946. London. National Gallery. Introduction by Leo Van Puyvelde

1949. Charleroi. XXIIIe Salon du Cercle Artistique et Littéraire de Charleroi. Text by Lucien Christophe, Paul Fierens, and Albert Croquez

1950. Venice. 25th Biennale. Text by Emile Langui

1951. Antwerp. Royal Museum of Fine Arts. Introduction by Walther Vanbeselaere

1951. New York, Museum of Modern Art; Boston, Institute of Contemporary Art; Cleveland, Museum of Art; St. Louis, City Art Museum. Text by Libby Tannenbaum

1954. Paris. Musée National d'Art Moderne. Text by Marcel Abraham, Jean Cassou, and Walther Vanbeselaere. See also *Arts* (Paris), March 2, 1954

CATALOGUES OF PRINTS

Garvens-Garvensburg, Herbert von. *James Ensor, Maler, Radierer, Komponist. Ein Hinweis mit dem vollständigen Katalog seines radierten Werkes*. Hanover, 1913

Delteil, Loys. "James Ensor," in *Le Peintre Graveur illustré*. vol. XIX. Paris, 1925

Avermaete, Roger. "James Ensor, der Graphiker," in *Der Cicerone* (Berlin), 1928

Dommartin, Henry. "Les Eaux-fortes de James Ensor," in *Le Flambeau* (Brussels), September-October 1930

Marx, Claude-Roger. "Les Eaux-fortes d'Ensor," in *L'Art Vivant* (Paris), July 1932

Croquez, Albert. *L'Oeuvre gravé de James Ensor. Catalogue raisonné*. Paris, 1935; Geneva, 1947

Lebeer, Louis. *Note pour servir de complément au catalogue de l'oeuvre gravé de James Ensor*. Brussels, 1939

Lebeer, Louis. *James Ensor aquafortiste*. (Monographies de l'art belge. Ser. 5, no. 5.) Antwerp, 1952

Van der Perre, Paul. "Quelques notes de portée pratique sur l'oeuvre gravé de James Ensor," in *Le Livre et l'Estampe* (Brussels), 1955

CHRONOLOGICAL LIST OF WORKS REPRODUCED

All the works reproduced are arranged by year, and within each year according to medium or technique. Measurements and owner's names are supplied wherever the information was available. Information for each reproduction is given in the following order: title; medium or technique; measurements (height before width); collection; page reference to reproduction or number in Classified Catalogue (c. c.). The *italic* numbers refer to color plates. The letter "c" preceding certain titles in this list means that the work is not dated but was probably executed during the year indicated.

1873 (?)

1. Boats at the Docks. – Oil on cardboard, $4^1/_8 \times 5^1/_8''$. Collection A. Croquez, Paris. c. c. 32

1876

2. View of the Flemish Plain. – Oil on cardboard, $9^3/_{16} \times 12^3/_8''$. Collection M. Mabille, Brussels. p. 29
3. Villa Albert. – Oil on cardboard, $9^1/_4 \times 6^1/_4''$. Collection G. Van Geluwe, Brussels. p. 235
4. Boat Aground, La Panne. – Oil on canvas, $7^1/_2 \times 9^1/_4''$. Collection Baron A. de Broqueville, Brussels. c. c. 34 (cf. replica c. c. 35)
5. Pole in the Dunes. – Oil on cardboard, $7^3/_8 \times 9^3/_8''$. Collection Ph. d'Arschot, Brussels. c. c. 44
6. Pole in the Dunes. – Oil on cardboard, $7^1/_2 \times 9^3/_8''$. Collection A. Croquez, Paris. c. c. 45
7. Dunes, Sea, and Ships. – Oil on cardboard, $7^1/_2 \times 9''$. Collection G. Van Geluwe, Brussels. c. c. 46 (cf. replica c. c. 47)
8. Landscape, Dunes. – Oil on canvas, $14^5/_8 \times 17^3/_4''$. Collection W. Willems, Brussels. c. c. 48
9. Dunes. – Oil on cardboard, $7^1/_4 \times 9^1/_4''$. Collection Claes-Boogaerts, Brussels. c. c. 49
10. Dunes. – Oil on cardboard, $7^1/_2 \times 9^3/_8''$. Collection A. Croquez, Paris. c. c. 50
11. The Flemish Plain Seen from the Dunes. – Oil on cardboard, $7^1/_4 \times 9^3/_8''$. Collection A. Croquez, Paris. c. c. 67

1877

12. Ostend Rooftops. – Oil on cardboard, $6^1/_4 \times 11^1/_2''$. Collection R. Lyr, Brussels. p. 236
13. (c) Bathing Cabin. – Oil on cardboard, $7^1/_2 \times 9^1/_4''$. Collection G. Van Geluwe, Brussels. p. 237
14. Model. – Oil on canvas, $25^1/_2 \times 22^3/_8''$. Collection M. E. Van den Bosch, Antwerp. p. 238
15. Triumphal Chariot. – Oil on canvas mounted on panel, $15 \times 19^1/_{16}''$. Collection M. Naessens, Brussels. p. 240
16. Seascape. – Oil on panel, $7^1/_8 \times 9^1/_2''$. Collection G. Van Geluwe, Brussels. c. c. 55
17. Calm Sea (or Bright Seascape). – Oil on canvas. $12^3/_8 \times 15^3/_4''$. Private collection. (Signed twice and dated 1880, but on the back February 28, 1877). c. c. 56
18. Estaminet. – Oil on cardboard, $7^1/_2 \times 9^1/_4''$. Collection G. Van Geluwe, Brussels. c. c. 68

19. (c) Outskirts of Blankenberghe. – Oil on cardboard, $7 \times 9^3/_{16}''$. Collection G. Van Geluwe, Brussels. c. c. 69
20. (c) Sailboat (after Turner). – Conté crayon, $6^5/_8 \times 8^5/_8''$. Royal Museum of Fine Arts, Antwerp. p. 134
21. Study (after Watteau). – Conté crayon, $6^5/_8 \times 8^5/_8''$. Royal Museum of Fine Arts, Antwerp. c. c. 220

1878

22. Judith and Holofernes. – Oil on canvas, $22^3/_8 \times 26^3/_8''$. Private collection. p. 241
23. (c) Shrimp Fishers. – Oil on panel, $4 \times 4^3/_4''$. Collection A. Frey, Brussels. c. c. 33
24. (c) Buoys on the Beach. – Oil on cardboard, $4 \times 5^1/_8''$. Collection G. Van Geluwe, Brussels. c. c. 51
25. (c) Water Gate near Ostend. – Oil on cardboard, $7^1/_8 \times 8^7/_8''$. Collection G. Van Geluwe, Brussels. c. c. 70
26. (c) Seascape. – Watercolor, $4^1/_8 \times 6^1/_8''$. Collection Claes-Boogaerts, Brussels. c. c. 36
27. (c) Old Woman with other Figures (after Rembrandt). – Conté crayon, $8^{11}/_{16} \times 6^1/_4''$. Royal Museum of Fine Arts, Antwerp. p. 134
28. (c) Sketch (after Goya). – Conté crayon, $8^3/_4 \times 6^3/_4''$. Royal Museum of Fine Arts, Antwerp. c. c. 222
29. (c) Troop of Soldiers (after Jacques Callot). – Pencil, $4^3/_4 \times 6^{11}/_{16}''$. Royal Museum of Fine Arts, Antwerp. c. c. 221

1879

30. Portrait of the Artist at the Easel. – Oil on canvas, $15^3/_4 \times 13''$. Collection R. Leten, Ghent. p. 21, p. 338 (detail) (cf. replica c. c. 21)
31. Girl with the Turned-up Nose. – Oil on canvas, $21^1/_4 \times 17^3/_4''$. Royal Museum of Fine Arts, Antwerp. p. 51 (detail), c. c. 1 (whole picture)
32. Self-Portrait. – Oil on panel, $7^7/_8 \times 5^3/_4''$. Collection A. Taevernier, Ghent. c. c. 19
33. Self-Portrait. – Oil on panel, $6^3/_4 \times 5^1/_8''$. Collection M. Mabille, Brussels. c. c. 20

1880

34. The Lamp Boy. – Oil on canvas, $59^1/_2 \times 35^3/_4''$. Royal Museums of Fine Arts, Brussels. p. 33 (cf. replica c. c. 239)
35. Lady with a Fan. – Oil on panel, $51^7/_8 \times 32^5/_8''$. Royal Museum of Fine Arts, Antwerp. p. 43
36. Rue de Flandre in the Snow. – Oil on canvas, $18^7/_8 \times 11^{13}/_{16}''$. Collection Colonel Louis Franck, London. p. 45
37. The Blue Flagon. – Oil on canvas, $17^3/_4 \times 19^5/_8''$. Collection G. Daelemans, Brussels. p. 59
38. Judas Flinging Pieces of Silver into the Temple. – Oil on canvas, $26^1/_8 \times 22^3/_8''$. Collection Claes-Boogaerts, p. 239
39. Sketch for 'Bourgeois Salon'. – Oil on canvas, $26 \times 21^5/_{16}''$. Collection G. Van Geluwe, Brussels. p. 242
40. Woman with Red Scarf. – Oil on canvas, $16^1/_8 \times 12^5/_8''$. Collection J. Speth, Antwerp. p. 243
41. (c) The Painter and his Model. – Oil on canvas, $14^1/_2 \times 18^7/_8''$. Museum, Tel Aviv. p. 251

42. (c) In the Woods. – Oil on canvas, $18^7/_8 \times 13^3/_4$". Museum, Tel Aviv. p. 252

43. The Colorist. – Oil on canvas, $40 \times 32^1/_4$". Collection Mme. J.-L. Wodon-Rousseau, Brussels. p. 254

44. Still Life (or The Bottles). – Oil on canvas. Private collection. p. 258

45. Lamps. – Oil on canvas, $14^1/_8 \times 17^3/_4$". Collection A. Croquez, Paris. p. 259

46. (c) Triptych. – Oil on panel. Formerly collection Mme. Ch. Franck, Antwerp. p. 260

47. The Painter Willy Finch on the Dunes. – Oil on panel, $10^5/_8 \times 13^3/_4$". Collection R. Leten, Ghent. c. c. 2

48. The Painter Willy Finch (or Vogels) in His Studio. – Oil on canvas, $20^1/_2 \times 16^1/_2$". Collection Mathijs, Ghent. c. c. 4

49. Head of the Painter Willy Finch. – Oil on canvas, $6^1/_4 \times 14^3/_4$". Private collection. c. c. 5

50. Gray Sea. – Oil on canvas, $23^1/_4 \times 29^1/_8$". Royal Museum of Fine Arts, Antwerp. c. c. 60

51. Pond with Poplars (or Park at Ostend). – Oil on canvas, $23^5/_8 \times 29^7/_8$". Museum, Tel Aviv. c. c. 63

52. Stream in the Woods. – Oil on canvas, $11^7/_8 \times 16^1/_2$". Museum, Tel Aviv. c. c. 64

53. The Stove. – Oil on canvas, $20^1/_2 \times 18^7/_8$". Collection Cl. Jussiant, Antwerp. c. c. 87

54. (c) Chinese Screen. – Oil on cardboard, $12^3/_8 \times 9$". Collection Mme. E. Lambotte, Antwerp. c. c. 91

55. (c) Still Life. – Oil on canvas, $11^7/_8 \times 18^7/_8$". Collection P. van der Perre, Brussels. c. c. 92

56. Chair with Fan. – Oil on cardboard, $7^1/_8 \times 9^3/_8$". Collection A. Croquez, Paris. c. c. 93

57. Blue and Pink Drapery. – Oil on canvas, $10^1/_4 \times 8^1/_4$". Collection J. Grubben, Brussels. c. c. 94

58. Still Life with Blue Chinoiseries. – Oil on canvas, $21^5/_8 \times 28^3/_8$". Private collection. c. c. 95

59. Still Life. – Oil on canvas, $22^3/_4 \times 26^3/_8$". Private collection. c. c. 102

60. Apples. – Oil on panel, $22^1/_4 \times 26^1/_8$". Collection Ghijselijns, Ghent. c. c. 103

61. Curly Cabbage. – Oil on canvas, $26^3/_8 \times 30^7/_8$". Royal Museums of Fine Arts, Brussels. c. c. 104 (cf. replica c. c. 105)

62. Silhouettes. – Gouache, $9^1/_2 \times 12^5/_8$". Collection A. Taevernier, Ghent, p. 136

63. (c) Silhouettes. – Gouache, $9^1/_2 \times 12^5/_8$". Royal Museums of Fine Arts, Brussels. p. 136

64. Silhouettes. – Gouache, $9^1/_2 \times 12^5/_8$". Private collection. p. 137

65. Silhouettes. – Gouache, $9^1/_2 \times 12^5/_8$". Private collection. p. 137

66. Figures. – Watercolor, $8^{13}/_{16} \times 13^3/_8$". Museum of Fine Arts, Ghent. p. 131

67. (c) Burlesque Figures. – Watercolor and charcoal, $7 \times 4^1/_8$". Collection G. Van Geluwe, Brussels, p. 141

68. Figures. – Watercolor, $12^5/_8 \times 9^1/_4$". Collection A. Croquez, Paris. c. c. 232

69. (c) Female Silhouettes. – Watercolor, $9^5/_8 \times 13$". Collection M. Mabille, Brussels. c. c. 233

70. (c) Figures. – Ink, $8^1/_4 \times 6^7/_8$". Collection Claes-Boogaerts, Brussels, p. 141

71. Seated Boy. – Black chalk, $28^3/_4 \times 23^3/_8$". Royal Museums of Fine Arts, Brussels. c. c. 213

72. (c) Draught Horses. – Charcoal and colored pencil, $8^7/_8 \times 6^7/_8$". Print Room, Brussels. p. 141

73. Young Sailor, Ostend. – Charcoal, $29^1/_2 \times 23^1/_4$". Collection Claes-Boogaerts, Brussels. p. 138

74. The Musicians. – Charcoal, $30 \times 23^3/_4$". Collection Mme. Van Weyenberg, Ressaix, Belgium. p. 139

75. Young Sailor. – Charcoal, $28^3/_4 \times 23^1/_4$". Collection Claes-Boogaerts, Brussels. c. c. 206

76. Ostend Boy. – Charcoal $29^1/_2 \times 23^1/_4$". Private collection. c. c. 207

77. Boy with Cap. – Charcoal, $28^3/_4 \times 23^1/_4$". Private collection. c. c. 208

78. Seated Man. – Charcoal, $28^3/_4 \times 23^1/_4$". Private collection. c. c. 209

79. Man Reading. – Charcoal, $29^1/_2 \times 22^1/_2$". Private collection. c. c. 210

80. Maidservant. – Charcoal, $29^1/_8 \times 23^1/_4$". Private collection. c. c. 211

81. Boy. – Charcoal, $29^1/_8 \times 20^1/_2$". Ensor Museum, Ostend. c. c. 212

82. (c) Portrait (after Frans Hals). – Charcoal, $8^3/_4 \times 6^3/_4$". Royal Museum of Fine Arts, Antwerp. c. c. 226

83. (c) Fiacre in Front of the Theater at Ostend. – Charcoal, $5^5/_{16} \times 8^3/_8$". Collection Claes-Boogaerts, Brussels. c. c. 228

84. (c) Page from a sketchbook. – Conté crayon, $8^{13}/_{16} \times 7$". Royal Museum of Fine Arts, Antwerp. c. c. 225

85. (c) Study. – Conté crayon, $8^{13}/_{16} \times 6^9/_{16}$". Royal Museum of Fine Arts, Antwerp. c. c. 227

86. (c) Sketch with Fisherman's Lantern. – Conté crayon, $8^1/_4 \times 10^1/_4$". Ensor Museum, Ostend. c. c. 230

87. (c) The Clock. – Pencil, $8^7/_8 \times 6^5/_8$". Collection A. Taevernier, Ghent. p. 19

88. (c) Boats. – Pencil, $5 \times 7^9/_{16}$". Print Room, Brussels. p. 30

89. (c) The Pilgrims at Emmaus (after Rembrandt). – Pencil. Whereabout unknow. p. 40

90. Old Horse. – Pencil, $6^5/_8 \times 8^5/_8$". Collection M. Mabille, Brussels. p. 133

91. (c) Study. – Pencil, $8 \times 6^1/_4$". Print Room, Brussels. p. 138

92. Portrait of a Man. – Pencil, $8^1/_2 \times 6^1/_4$". Collection Claes-Boogaerts, Brussels. p. 138

93. Man with a Pan. – Pencil, $29^1/_8 \times 24$". Museum, Tel Aviv. p. 139

94. Young Woman Seated. – Pencil, $29^7/_8 \times 24^3/_8$". Museum Tel Aviv. p. 139

95. King Pest. – Pencil, $6^5/_8 \times 8^5/_8$". Formerly collection Manteau, Brussels. p. 147

96. Portrait of Mme. Ernest Rousseau. – Pencil, $9^5/_8 \times 7^1/_2$". Collection Claes-Boogaerts, Brussels. c. c. 3

97. (c) Landscape with Church (after Constable). – Pencil, $6^{11}/_{16} \times 8^5/_8$". Royal Museum of Fine Arts, Antwerp. c. c. 71

98. (c) Dog (after Rembrandt). – Pencil, $5^3/_4 \times 6^1/_2$". Collection Claes-Boogaerts, Brussels. c. c. 223

99. (c) Page from a sketchbook. – Pencil, $8^{13}/_{16} \times 6^5/_8$". Royal Museum of Fine Arts, Antwerp. c. c. 224

100. (c) The Cart. – Pencil, $3^3/_4 \times 4^7/_8$". Royal Museums of Fine Arts, Brussels. c. c. 229

101. (c) Figures. – Pencil, $8^1/_4 \times 6^1/_8$". Collection Claes-Boogaerts, Brussels. c. c. 234

102. (c) Sketch. – Pencil, $6^3/_4 \times 8^3/_4$". Collection Claes-Boogaerts, Brussels. c. c. 236

103. Portrait of the Artist's Father. – Oil on canvas, $39^1/_4 \times 31^1/_2$". Royal Museums of Fine Arts, Brussels. p. 25

1881

104. Rue de Flandre in the Sun. – Oil on canvas, 42×33". Collection J. Speth, Antwerp. p. 47

105. Afternoon at Ostend. – Oil on canvas, $42^3/_4 \times 53$". Royal Museum of Fine Arts, Antwerp. p. 53 (whole picture), p. 55 (detail) (cf. 1910 painting p. 222)

106. Somber Lady. – Oil on canvas, $39^1/_4 \times 31^1/_2$". Royal Museums of Fine Arts, Brussels. p. 57

107. Woman with Blue Scarf. – Oil on canvas, 26³/₄ × 23″. Royal Museum of Fine Arts, Antwerp. p. 244

108. Bourgeois Salon. – Oil on canvas, 52 × 42¹/₂″. Royal Museum of Fine Arts, Antwerp. p. 248

109. Russian Music. – Oil on canvas, 52¹/₄ × 43″. Royal Museums of Fine Arts, Brussels. p. 249

110. Woman in Blue. – Oil on canvas, 23¹/₄ × 27¹/₈″. Royal Museums of Fine Arts, Brussels. p. 255

111. Pears. – Oil on canvas, 15³/₄ × 19⁵/₈″. Collection Mme. P. Buyssens, Brussels. p. 260

112. Wool-Carder. – Oil on canvas, 23³/₈ × 15³/₄″. Formerly collection Mme. Ch. Franck, Antwerp. c. c. 6

113. Meats. (Destroyed during World War II). – Oil on canvas, 31¹/₈ × 38⁵/₈″. Formerly Ensor Museum, Ostend. c. c. 106

114. Hunters in Winter (sheet from a notebook). – Conté crayon, 8³/₄ × 6¹³/₁₆″. Royal Museum of Fine Arts, Ant-

115. werp. c. c. 235
(c) Lamp. – Pencil, 8¹/₂ × 6¹/₄″. Collection A. Taevernier, Ghent. p. 140

116. Woman Sewing. – Pencil, 9 × 7″. Collection Claes-Boogaerts, Brussels. p. 143

1882

117. The Painter Willy Finch. – Oil on canvas, 43³/₁₆ × 37⁵/₁₆″. Collection J. Janssen, Antwerp. p. 63 (detail), c. c. 7

118. Portrait of the Artist's Mother. – Oil on canvas, 39⁵/₁₆ × 31¹/₂″. Royal Museums of Fine Arts, Brussels. p. 245

119. Portrait of Willy Finch. – Oil on canvas, 19¹/₂ × 11⁵/₈″. Royal Museum of Fine Arts, Antwerp. p. 247

120. Waiting. – Oil on canvas, 25¹/₂ × 20¹/₂″. Royal Museum of Fine Arts, Antwerp. p. 250

121. Woman Eating Oysters. – Oil on canvas, 81¹/₂ × 59¹/₁₆″. Royal Museum of Fine Arts, Antwerp. p. 256 (cf. light version p. 257)

122. Oysters. – Oil on canvas, 31 × 39″. Royal Museum of Fine Arts, Antwerp. p. 261

123. The Skate. – Oil on canvas, 31¹/₂ × 39¹/₄″. Royal Museum of Fine Arts, Antwerp. p. 261

124. (c) The Cab. – Oil on canvas, 16³/₈ × 22″. Collection A. Taevernier, Ghent. p. 262

125. Sick Tramp Warming Himself. (Destroyed during World War II). – Oil on canvas, 38¹/₂ × 34⁵/₈″. Formerly Ensor Museum, Ostend. p. 263 (cf. p. 183 and c. c. 240)

126. Lady in Distress. – Oil on canvas, 39¹/₄ × 31¹/₂″. The Louvre (Jeu de Paume), Paris. p. 264

127. Lady with Red Umbrella. – Oil on canvas, 20¹/₂ × 14³/₁₆″. Royal Museum of Fine Arts, Antwerp. c. c. 8

128. Portrait of Théo Hannon. – Oil on canvas, 27¹/₈ × 19¹/₄″. Royal Museum of Fine Arts, Antwerp, c. c. 9

129. The Breakwater. – Oil on canvas, 17¹/₂ × 21⁷/₈″. Collection G. Van Geluwe, Brussels. c. c. 57

130. The White Cloud. – Oil on canvas, 31¹/₂ × 39″. Royal Museum of Fine Arts, Antwerp. c. c. 59

131. (c) Seascape. – Oil on canvas, 8⁵/₈ × 13³/₈″. Museum, Tel Aviv. c. c. 61

132. Cottages on the Dunes. – Oil on canvas, 12⁵/₈ × 15³/₈″. Collection Van Gelder, Brussels. c. c. 73

133. Street at Ostend. – Oil on panel, 11 × 7″. Collection P. H., Brussels, c. c. 79

134. Seashells and Chinoiseries. – Oil on canvas, 31⁷/₈ × 39¹/₄″. Formerly collection M. Mabille, Brussels. c. c. 107

135. Working the Fields. – Black chalk, 4⁷/₈ × 6⁷/₈″. Print Room, Brussels. c. c. 72

136. Glass. – Charcoal, 8 × 5⁷/₈″. Collection Claes-Boogaerts, Brussels. p. 140

137. (c) Glasses. – Charcoal, 8⁵/₈ × 6⁵/₈″. Collection Claes-Boogaerts, Brussels. p. 140

138. (c) Attributes of the Studio. – Pencil, 8¹/₄ × 6⁵/₈″. Collection A. Taevernier, Ghent. p. 140

139. Susanna and the Elders. – Colored pencil, 8⁵/₈ × 6⁵/₈″. Collection Mme. S. Janson-Hallet, Rhode-St.-Genèse, Belgium. c. c. 188

140. (c) Head of a Woman. – Pencil, 8 × 6¹/₄″. Collection M. Hendrickx, Brussels. c. c. 214

141. (c) Sleeping Woman. – Pencil, 8⁷/₈ × 6¹/₂″. Collection G. Van Geluwe, Brussels. c. c. 215

1883

142. Portrait of the Painter in a Flowered Hat. – Oil on canvas, 30¹/₁₆ × 24³/₁₆″. Ensor Museum, Ostend. p. 17 (detail), c. c. 22 (whole picture)

143. The Rower. – Oil on canvas, 31 × 38⁷/₈″. Royal Museum of Fine Arts, Antwerp. p. 35

144. The Drunkards. – Oil on canvas, 45³/₁₆ × 64³/₄″. Collection L. Bogaerts, Brussels. p. 185

145. Scandalized Masks. – Oil on canvas, 53 × 44¹⁵/₁₆″. Royal Museums of Fine Arts, Brussels. p. 287 (cf. etching p. 126)

146. (c) Umbrella. – Charcoal, 8⁵/₈ × 6⁵/₈″. Collection Claes-Boogaerts, Brussels. c. c. 231

147. Gamblers. – Pencil. Whereabout unknown. p. 26 (cf. etching p. 124)

148. Writing Woman (the artist's sister). – Pencil, 8¹/₄ × 11⁷/₁₆″. Ensor Museum, Ostend. p. 142

149. Self-Portrait. – Pencil. Private collection. p. 337

150. Self-Portrait. – Pencil, 8⁵/₈ × 6³/₄″. Collection M. Mabille, Brussels. c. c. 23

151. (c) The Artist's Sister. – Pencil sketch, 8³/₄ × 6³/₄″. Collection Claes-Boogaerts, Brussels. c. c. 216

152. (c) Sleep (sheet of studies). – Pencil, 8³/₄ × 6¹/₄″. Collection Claes-Boogaerts, Brussels. c. c. 217

153. (c) Portrait. – Pencil, 8 × 6¹/₄″. Royal Museums of Fine Arts, Brussels. c. c. 218

154. (c) Child Drawing. – Pencil, 8⁵/₈ × 6¹/₄″. Collection G. Van Geluwe, Brussels. c. c. 219

1884

155. Portrait of Dario de Regoyos. – Oil on canvas, 26³/₄ × 22³/₄″. Private collection. p. 246 (cf. 1888 drawing p. 138)

156. Ostend Rooftops. – Oil on canvas, 61³/₄ × 82³/₈. Royal Museum of Fine Arts, Antwerp. p. 253 (cf. 1906 replica c. c. 84)

157. Child with Doll. – Oil on canvas, 59¹/₁₆ × 35³/₄″. Museum Wallraf-Richartz (Collection Haubrich), Cologne. p. 266

158. Interior (The Rousseau Drawing Room, Rue Vautier, Brussels). – Oil on canvas, 23⁵/₈ × 31¹/₂″. Collection A. V. G. Pirson, Brussels. p. 268

1885

159. Skeleton Looking at Chinoiseries. – Oil on canvas, 39¹/₄ × 23⁵/₈″. Collection L. Bogaerts, Brussels. p. 221

160. Flowers in a Bucket (or Fanfare in Red). – Oil on canvas, 43¹/₂ × 29⁷/₈″. Private collection. p. 267

161. Ostend Rooftops. – Oil on canvas, 43 × 52⁵/₈″. Collection Colonel L. Franck, C. B. E., London. p. 276

162. Hôtel de Ville, Brussels. – Oil on canvas, 39¹/₄ × 29⁷/₈″. Museum of Fine Arts, Liège. p. 277

163. Lighthouse at Ostend. – Oil on canvas, 24⁵/₈ × 29¹/₂″. Royal Museums of Fine Arts, Brussels. c. c. 52

164. (c) Dunes and Calm Sea. – Oil on cardboard, $7^3/_8 \times 9^3/_8''$. Collection G. Van Geluwe, Brussels. c. c. 53

165. Sunset over the Sea. – Oil on canvas, $44 \times 63''$. Collection Baron H. de Broqueville, Brussels. c. c. 58

166. Still Life: The Hare. – Oil on canvas, $28^3/_8 \times 34^5/_8''$. Collection Cl. Jussiant, Antwerp. c. c. 108

167. Haunted Furniture. (Destroyed during World War II). – Oil on canvas, $35 \times 40^1/_2''$. Formerly Ensor Museum, Ostend. c. c. 127

168. (c) Woman at a Café Table (after Degas). – Conté crayon, $8^{11}/_{16} \times 6^{11}/_{16}''$. Royal Museum of Fine Arts, Antwerp. p. 134

169. Chinoiseries. – Conté crayon, $8^{11}/_{16} \times 6^7/_8''$. Royal Museum of Fine Arts, Antwerp. p. 135

170. (c) Silhouette of an Incroyable (after Grévin). – Conté crayon, $8^3/_4 \times 6^7/_8''$. Royal Museum of Fine Arts, Antwerp. p. 135

171. (c) Grotesque Figure. – Conté crayon, $8^3/_4 \times 6^7/_8''$. Royal Museum of Fine Arts, Antwerp. p. 135

172. (c) Self-Portrait. – Charcoal, $8^5/_8 \times 11''$. Collection Claes-Boogaerts, Brussels. p. 142

173. Hail Jesus, King of the Jews. – Charcoal and pencil, $76^5/_8 \times 55''$. Print Room, Brussels. p. 150

174. Haunted Mantlepiece. – Pencil, $8^7/_8 \times 6^7/_8''$. Private Collection. p. 144

175. (c) Portrait of My Mother. – Pencil, $11^7/_{16} \times 8^3/_{16}''$. Collection G. Van Geluwe, Brussels. p. 145

176. Self-Portrait. – Pencil, $8 \times 5^7/_8''$. Collection M. Mabille, Brussels. p. 75, p. 338 (detail)

177. (c) Sheet of Self-Portrait sketches. – Pencil. Collection Mme. J.-L. Wodon-Rousseau, Brussels. c. c. 24

178. The Cruel: Jesus Presented to the People. – Pencil, $59 \times 39^1/_4''$. Collection Claes-Boogaerts, Brussels. c. c. 189

179. (c) Don Quixote. – Colored pencil, $5^3/_8 \times 6^5/_8''$. Collection Claes-Boogaerts, Brussels. c. c. 238

1886

180. The Descent from the Cross. – Oil on panel, $23^5/_8 \times 18^1/_2''$. Collection Claes-Boogaerts, Brussels, p. 146

181. Children Dressing. – Oil on canvas, $53 \times 43^1/_4''$. Collection Cl. Jussiant, Antwerp. p. 265

182. Landscape. – Oil on canvas, $24^3/_8 \times 30^3/_4''$. Collection B. Goldschmidt, Brussels. c. c. 74

183. The Cathedral. Etching, $9^1/_2 \times 7^1/_2''$. p. 113

184. The Adoration of the Shepherds. – Black chalk and charcoal on paper pasted on canvas, $29^1/_2 \times 23^5/_8''$. Royal Museums of Fine Arts, Brussels. c. c. 192

185. Futurist Dream. – Conté crayon, $8^5/_8 \times 11^5/_8''$. Private collection. p. 147

186. In the Shadow (detail). – Conté crayon, Collection Claes-Boogaerts, Brussels. p. 338

187. Self-Portrait (later titled My Portrait Sad and Sumptuous). Pencil, $8^3/_4 \times 6^1/_4''$. Collection Claes-Boogaerts, p. 335

188. Ensor and His Family. – Pencil, $8^1/_4 \times 11^7/_{16}''$. Collection M. Hendrickx, Brussels. p. 142

189. Christ Driving the Money Changers from the Temple. – Pencil, $9^1/_{16} \times 6^5/_8''$. Collection A. Taevernier, Ghent. p. 151

190. Boats. – Colored pencil, $6^3/_4 \times 8^3/_4''$. Print Room, Brussels. c. c. 37

191. The Artist Decomposed. – Colored pencil, $4^7/_8 \times 3^1/_4''$. National Museum of Modern Art, Paris. c. c. 128

192. Calvary. – Pencil and color on panel, $6^3/_4 \times 8^3/_4''$. Collection Claes-Boogaerts, Brussels. c. c. 190

193. The Dead Christ Watched Over by Angels. – Pencil, $5^7/_8 \times 8''$. Collection M. Mabille, Brussels. c. c. 191

1887

194. The Tribulations of Saint Anthony. – Oil on canvas, $45^7/_8 \times 65^5/_8''$. Museum of Modern Art, New York. p. 77

195. Carnival on the Beach. – Oil on canvas, $21^5/_8 \times 25^1/_2''$. Royal Museums of Fine Arts, Brussels. p. 103

196. Study of Light (or Adam and Eve Driven from Paradise). – Oil on canvas, $80^3/_4 \times 96^1/_2''$. Royal Museums of Fine Arts, Brussels. p. 241

197. The Adoration of the Shepherds. – Oil on Panel, $18^3/_8 \times 23^3/_4''$. Collection Th. Léger, Brussels. c. c. 193

198. Portrait of Ernest Rousseau. – Etching, $9^1/_2 \times 7^1/_8''$. p. 114

199. Ostend Docks. – Etching, $3^1/_2 \times 5^1/_{16}''$. p. 115

200. Devils' Sabbath. – Etching, $8^5/_8 \times 10^1/_2''$. p. 122

201. The Large View of Mariakerke. – Etching, $8^1/_2 \times 10^5/_8''$. c. c. 75

202. My Father on His Deathbed. – Pencil, $6^5/_8 \times 8^{13}/_{16}''$. Private collection. p. 354

1888

203. Christ in Agony. – Oil on panel, $6^1/_4 \times 8^1/_4''$. Collection M. Mabille, Brussels. p. 78

204. Garden of Love. – Oil on canvas, $37^3/_4 \times 44''$. Collection Cl. Jussiant, Antwerp. p. 83 (detail), c. c. 182 (whole picture)

205. The Entry of Christ into Brussels. – Oil on canvas, $101^5/_{16} \times 149^1/_4''$. Collection Colonel L. Franck, C. B. E., London (on loan in the Royal Museum of Fine Arts, Antwerp). p. 181 (detail), pp. 274/275 (whole picture)

206. Masks Confronting Death. – Oil on canvas, $31^1/_2 \times 39^1/_4''$. Collection G. Van Geluwe, Brussels. p. 292

207. The Tower of Lisseweghe. – Oil on canvas, $24 \times 28^3/_4''$. Private collection. c. c. 76

208. The Great Basin at Ostend. – Etching, $7 \times 9^1/_4''$. p. 115

209. Grove. – Etching, $3^{15}/_{16} \times 5^1/_2''$. p. 116

210. Woods at Groenendael. – Etching, $4^5/_8 \times 3^1/_8''$. p. 116

211. Skull and Masks. – Etching, $3^7/_8 \times 5^3/_8''$. p. 118

212. Odd Insects (the artist and Mme. Ernest Rousseau). – Etching, $4^5/_8 \times 6^1/_4''$. p. 118

213. Murder. – Etching, $7 \times 9^3/_8''$. p. 119

214. Gendarmes. – Etching, $7 \times 9^5/_{16}''$. p. 119

215. Capture of a Strange City. – Etching, $6^7/_8 \times 9^5/_{16}''$. p. 120

216. Cataclysms. – Etching, $7 \times 9^3/_8''$. p. 121

217. Combat of Demons. – Etching, $10^3/_8 \times 12^1/_8''$. p. 122

218. Boats on the Beach. – Etching, $7 \times 9^3/_8''$. p. 130 (cf. 1892 painting p. 107 and 1900 painting p. 273)

219. My Portrait in 1960. – Etching, $2^{11}/_{16} \times 4^{11}/_{16}''$. p. 206

220. The Harbor of Ostend. – Etching, $3^1/_8 \times 4^5/_8''$. c. c. 38

221. Boats. Etching, $6^7/_8 \times 9^1/_4''$. c. c. 39

222. Wind. – Etching, $6^7/_8 \times 9^3/_4''$. c. c. 65

223. Path at Groenendael. – Etching, $5^3/_8 \times 4''$. c. c. 77

224. Hôtel de Ville, Oudenaarde. – Etching, $6^1/_4 \times 4^5/_8''$. c. c. 80

225. The Street Lamp. – Etching, $3^3/_4 \times 2^3/_4''$ c. c. 81

226. (c) The Devil in the Belfry. – Conté crayon, $8^5/_8 \times 6^5/_8''$. Collection Mme. J. Demany, Brussels. p. 148

227. Carnival at Brussels. – Conté crayon, $8^5/_8 \times 6^5/_8''$. Collection G. Bolle, Brussels. p. 149

228. Christ in Agony. – Charcoal and pencil, $23^3/_8 \times 29^1/_8''$. Royal Museums of Fine Arts, Brussels. p. 151 (cf. 1895 etching p. 125)

229. The Guitarist. – Pencil, $8^1/_2 \times 6^1/_2''$. Collection Claes-Boogaerts, Brussels. p. 138 (cf. 1884 painting p. 246)

230. Demons Tormenting Me. – Black pencil with colored pencil, $8^5/_8 \times 11^3/_4''$. Collection Claes-Boogaerts, Brussels. p. 336 (cf. 1895 etching p. 124)

231. Page of the catalogue of the exhibition of Les XX, 1888. Each page of the catalogue reproduced the writing and drawing of an exhibiting artist. p. 342

1889

232. Still Life with Fruits. – Oil on canvas, 22³/₄ × 28⁵/₁₆″. Collection Barones Lambert, Brussels. p. 70
233. Fall of the Rebellious Angels. – Oil on canvas, 42³/₈ × 51⁷/₈″ Royal Museum of Fine Arts, Antwerp. p. 79
234. Old Woman with Masks (also called The Theater of Masks and Bouquet d'Artifice). – Oil on canvas, 21¹/₄ × 18¹/₂″. Collection R. Leten, Ghent. p. 89 (detail), c. c. 129 (whole picture)
235. Attributes of the Studio. – Oil on canvas, 32⁵/₈ × 44⁵/₁₆″. Collection R. Leten, Ghent, p. 97
236. Astonishment of the Mask Wouse. – Oil on canvas, 42³/₄ × 51¹/₂″. Royal Museum of Fine Arts. Antwerp. p. 169
237. Skeletons Trying to Warm Themselves (or No Fire, Will You get some tomorrow?). – Oil on canvas, 25¹/₅ × 18″. Private collection, Texas, USA. p. 171
238. Small Fruits. – Oil on panel, 7¹/₂ × 10¹/₄″. Private collection. c. c. 109
239. (c) Flowers and Fruits. – Oil on canvas, 19³/₄ × 23⁵/₈″. Collection A. Taevernier, Ghent. c. c. 121
240. Theater of Masks. – Oil on canvas, 23¹/₄ × 28³/₈″. Royal Museum of Fine Arts, Antwerp. c. c. 171
241. Kermess at the Windmill. – Etching, 5³/₈ × 7″. p. 117
242. My Portrait Skeletonized. – Etching, 4³/₄ × 3¹/₁₆″. c. c. 25
243. Peste dessous, peste dessus, peste partout. – Pencil and red chalk, 8⁵/₈ × 11³/₄″. Collection A. Taevernier, Ghent. c. c. 149 (cf. photograph p. 344)
244. (c) Belgium in the Nineteenth Century. – Pencil and colored pencil, 6³/₈ × 8¹/₂″. Print Room, Brussels. p. 152
245. View of Ostend. – Pencil on panel, 8⁵/₈ × 6¹/₂″. Collection Claes-Boogaerts, Brussels. c. c. 82
246. (c) Roman Triumph. – Pencil and colored pencil on panel, 14⁵/₈ × 18¹/₈″. Print Room, Brussels. c. c. 156

1890

247. Intrigue. – Oil on canvas, 35³/₈ × 58⁷/₈″. Royal Museum of Fine Arts, Antwerp. p. 85 (whole picture), p. 86 (detail), p. 87 (detail) (cf. 1911 replica c. c. 134)
248. Ensor and General Leman Discussing Painting. – Oil on panel, 4³/₄ × 6¹/₄″. Collection M. Mabille, Brussels. p. 111 (whole picture), p. 339 (detail)
249. Portrait of Emile Verhaeren. – Oil on panel, 9³/₈ × 7³/₁₆″. Royal Bibliotheque, Brussels. p. 208
250. The Embroiderer. – Oil on panel, 18³/₁₆ × 14¹/₂″. Collection J. Beuckeleers, Antwerp. p. 269
251. Forbidding Figure (portrait of the Artist's Aunt). – Oil on panel, 9⁵/₈ × 7¹/₂″. Collection M. Mabille, Brussels. p. 217
252. Boats. – Oil on canvas, 24³/₈ × 26³/₄″. Royal Museum of Fine Arts, Antwerp. p. 272
253. Still Life with Blue Pot. – Oil on panel, 15 × 18¹/₁₆″. Museum Kröller-Müller, Otterlo, Holland. p. 280
254. Still Life. – Oil on canvas. Private collection. p. 281
255. Murder. – Oil on canvas, 22³/₄ × 29¹/₂″. Collection S. Salz, New York. p. 291
256. (c) Ostend. – Oil on canvas, 12⁵/₈ × 15³/₄″. Museum, Tel Aviv. c. c. 40
257. The Basin at Ostend. – Oil on canvas, 22⁴/₅ × 28³/₄″. Royal Museum of Fine Arts, Antwerp. c. c. 41
258. The Domain of Arnheim. – Oil on canvas, 31¹/₂ × 39¹/₄″. Collection Baron R. Boël, Brussels. c. c. 66

259. Street at Ostend. – Oil on canvas, 28³/₄ × 19¹/₂″. Private collection. c. c. 83
260. (c) Remorse of the Corsican Ogre. – Oil on panel, 6¹/₄ × 8¹/₄″. Collection M. Mabille, Brussels. c. c. 144
261. Portrait of the Artist at the Easel (detail). – Oil on canvas, 37⁵/₁₆ × 16¹/₄″. Royal Museum of Fine Arts, Antwerp. p. 338
262. Music, Rue de Flandre. – Etching, 3¹/₈ × 4⁵/₈″. p. 39 (cf. 1891 painting p. 49)
263. (c) People Sticking Out Their Tongues. – Gouache on cardboard, 13³/₈ × 19⁵/₈″. Collection A. Taevernier, Ghent. p. 284
264. (c) Sloth. – Pencil, 8⁷/₁₆ × 11³/₈″. Collection G. de Groof, Brussels. p. 64
265. (c) Cathedral. – Colored pencil. Whereabout unknown. p. 154
266. White and Red Clowns Evolving. – Colored pencil, 9¹/₂ × 11¹/₂″. Collection B. Goldschmidt, Brussels. p. 157
267. (c) Self-Portrait. – Pencil, 28³/₄ × 21⁵/₁₆″. Royal Museums of Fine Arts, Brussels. c. c. 26
268. (c) Masks Confronting Death. – Colored pencil, 9⁷/₈ × 13³/₈″. Royal Museums of Fine Arts, Brussels. c. c. 131 (cf. 1897 painting p. 167)
269. Napoleon at Waterloo. – Pencil 8⁷/₈ × 6¹/₂″. Collection G. Van Geluwe, Brussels. c. c. 143

1891

270. Music, Rue de Flandre. – Oil on panel. 9⁷/₁₆ × 7¹/₂″. Royal Museum of Fine Arts, Antwerp. p. 49 (cf. 1890 etching p. 39)
271. Christ Calming the Water. – Oil on canvas, 30⁵/₈ × 38¹/₂″. Ensor Museum, Ostend. p. 104
272. Grotesque Singers. – Oil on canvas, 6¹/₄ × 8¹/₂″. Collection M. Mabille, Brussels. p. 172
273. The Animal Musicians (or The Tragic Musicians). – Oil on panel, 6¹/₄ × 8¹/₄″. Collection Baron Ch. Janssen, Brussels. p. 173
274. Skeletons Fighting for the Body of a Hanged Man. – Oil on canvas, 23¹/₄ × 29¹/₈″. Royal Museum of Fine Arts, Antwerp. p. 175 (detail), c. c. 130 (whole picture).
275. Skeletons Disputing a Herring. – Oil on panel, 6¹/₁₆ × 8¹/₄″. Collection B. Goldschmidt, Brussels. p. 192
276. The Judges. – Oil on panel, 15 × 18¹/₈″. Collection P. de Weissenbruch, Brussels. p. 196
277. Man of Sorrows. – Oil on panel, 8¹/₂ × 6¹/₄″. Collection R. Leten, Ghent. p. 199
278. Ecce Homo or Christ and His Critics. – Oil on panel, 4³/₄ × 6¹/₄. Collection Mme. Marteaux, Brussels. p. 201 (whole picture), p. 339 (detail)
279. Egg, Crab, and Shrimps (or The Soft-boiled Egg). – Oil on panel, 4³/₄ × 6¹/₄″. Collection J. Stoclet, Brussels. p. 280
280. Garden of Love. – Oil on canvas, 29¹/₂ × 39¹/₄″. Collection Mme. Sacher-Stehlin, Basel. p. 284
281. Baptism with Masks. – Oil on panel, 7¹/₂ × 9¹/₂″. Collection Claes-Boogaerts, Brussels. p. 288
282. Masquerade. – Oil on panel, 7¹/₂ × 9¹/₂″. Collection R. Rothschild, Brussels. p. 288
283. (c) Still Life. – Oil on canvas, 39³/₈ × 30³/₄″. Royal Museum of Fine Arts, Antwerp. c. c. 96
284. Philip II in Hell. – Oil on panel, 4³/₈ × 5⁷/₈″. Collection P. Rossel, Brussels. c. c. 150
285. Christ in Hell. – Pencil, 8³/₄ × 11³/₄″. Collection G. de Groof, Brussels. p. 154
286. The Cuirassiers at Waterloo (or Napoleon's Last Stand). – Indian Ink and pastel, 8¹³/₁₆ × 24¹/₂″. Royal Museum of Fine Arts, Antwerp. p. 229

287. Battle of the Golden Spurs. – Colored pencil and ink on panel, $12^3/_4 \times 17^7/_8''$. Royal Museums of Fine Arts, Brussels. c. c. 157 (cf. 1895 etching p. 123)

1892

288. The Dispair of Pierrot. – Oil on canvas, $56^{15}/_{16} \times 76^9/_{16}''$. Collection G. Daelemans, Brussels. p. 91 (cf. replica c. c. 132)

289. (c) Boats on the Beach. – Oil on canvas, $19^5/_8 \times 35^3/_8''$. Collection G. Van Geluwe, Brussels. p. 107 (cf. 1900 painting p. 273 und 1888 etching p. 130)

290. Melancholy Fishwives. – Oil on canvas, $39^1/_4 \times 31^1/_2''$ Private collection, Texas, USA. p. 187

291. Consoling Virgin. – Oil on canvas, $18^7/_8 \times 15''$. Collection A. Taevernier, Ghent. pp. 203, 339 (details), c. c. 196

292. The Skate. – Oil on canvas, $31^1/_2 \times 39^1/_4''$. Royal Museums of Fine Arts, Brussels. p. 278

293. Curly Cabbage. – Oil on canvas, $31^7/_8 \times 39^1/_4''$. Collection Ph. Dotremont, Brussels. p. 279

294. Strange Masks. – Oil on canvas, $39^1/_4 \times 31^1/_2''$. Royal Museums of Fine Arts, Brussels. p. 286

295. Monsieur and Madame Ernest Rousseau Talking with Sophie Yoteko. – Oil on panel, $4^{11}/_{16} \times 6^1/_4''$. Collection Mme. J. Demany, Brussels. p. 289

296. Duel of Masks. – Oil on canvas, $15^3/_8 \times 24''$. Collection Dhéry, Brussels. p. 293

297. My Favorite Room. – Oil on canvas, $31^1/_2 \times 39^3/_8''$. Museum, Tel Aviv. c. c. 88

298. Flowers. – Oil on panel, $10^5/_8 \times 17^3/_4''$. Collection B. Goldschmidt, Brussels. c. c. 122

299. The Strike. – Pastel, $13^3/_8 \times 26^3/_4''$. Collection G. Van Geluwe, Brussels. c. c. 146

300. Christ Mocked. – Pen, $4^3/_4 \times 5^7/_8''$. Collection Claes-Boogaerts, Brussels. c. c. 194

301. The Sermon of St. Babilas. – Colored pencil on panel, $18^1/_8 \times 15''$. Formerly collection M. Mabille, Brussels. p. 152

302. (c) Fishermen's Strike at Ostend (or Gendarmes Firing at Fishermen). – Pencil, $6^1/_4 \times 8^1/_2''$. Collection Claes-Boogaerts, Brussels. c. c. 145

303. The Rout of the Mercenaries. – Pencil, $6^1/_4 \times 8^1/_2''$. Collection M. Mabille, Brussels. c. c. 158

304. The Elephants' Ball. – Pencil $4^3/_8 \times 5^7/_8''$. Collection Claes-Boogaerts, Brussels. c. c. 159

305. Joan of Arc. – Colored pencil, $11^7/_8 \times 9^1/_{16}''$. Collection Mme. Storck-Hertoge, Brussels. c. c. 195

306. (c) Joshua Comments the Sun. – Pencil, $6^5/_8 \times 8^7/_8''$. Collection Claes-Boogaerts, Brussels. c. c. 197

1893

307. Portrait of Eugène Demolder. – Oil on panel, $14^1/_8 \times 8^1/_4''$. Collection M. Mabille, Brussels. p. 270

308. Still Life. – Oil on canvas, $22^3/_8 \times 27^1/_2''$. Collection A. Croquez, Paris, p. 281

309. Pierrot and Skeleton in Yellow Robe. – Oil on panel, $15 \times 18^7/_8''$. Collection J. de Lange, Antwerp. p. 294

310. (c) Curly Cabbage. – Oil on canvas, $31^7/_8 \times 39^1/_4''$. Private collection. c. c. 105 (cf. 1880 painting c. c. 104)

311. (c) Still Life. – Oil on canvas, $31^1/_4 \times 39^1/_4''$. Museum of Fine Arts, Liège. c. c. 110

312. (c) Old Woman Asleep. – Pencil, $8^5/_8 \times 11^7/_8''$. Collection B. Goldschmidt, Brussels. p. 69

1894

313. Masks Watching a Turtle. – Oil on canvas, $8^5/_8 \times 9^9/_{16}''$. Collection Barones Lambert, Brussels. p. 289

314. Gathering of Skeletons. – Oil on Canvas, $7^7/_8 \times 14^1/_{16}''$. Private collection. p. 292

315. Shrimp. – Oil on panel. Private collection. c. c. 111

1895

316. Seashells. – Oil on canvas, $31^{13}/_{16} \times 39^1/_4''$. Collection S. Salz, New York, p. 71

317. (c) Symphony in Light. – Oil on panel, $6^1/_2 \times 9^1/_2''$. Collection G. Van Geluwe, Brussels. p. 282

318. (c) Still Life with Peaches. – Oil on panel, $7^1/_2 \times 9^1/_4''$. Collection M. Mabille, Brussels. p. 282

319. Fish. – Oil on canvas, $27^7/_8 \times 36^1/_4$. Collection Cl. Jussiant, Antwerp. c. c. 112

320. Ballet Dancers. – Oil on canvas, $11^7/_8 \times 15^3/_4''$. Formerly collection Ed. Hannon, Brussels. c. c. 169 (cf. 1908 replica c. c. 170)

321. The Battle of the Golden Spurs. – Etching, $9^1/_2 \times 11''$. p. 123 (cf. 1891 drawing c. c. 157)

322. Gamblers. – Etching, $4^5/_8 \times 6^1/_4''$. p. 124 (cf. 1883 drawing p. 26)

323. Demons Tormenting Me. – Etching $5^5/_8 \times 7^3/_4''$. p. 124 (cf. 1888 drawing p. 336)

324. Christ Tormented by Demons. – Etching, $7 \times 9^1/_2''$. p. 125 (cf. 1888 drawing p. 151)

325. Christ Among the Beggars. – Etching, $3^{11}/_{16} \times 5^7/_8''$. p. 125

326. Scandalized Masks. – Etching, $4^{11}/_{16} \times 3^1/_4''$. p. 126 (cf. 1883 painting p. 287)

327. The Descent of Christ into Hell. – Etching, $5^1/_2 \times 7''$. p. 176

328. The Bad Doctors. – Colored etching, $7 \times 9^7/_8''$. Collection A. Taevernier, Ghent. p. 193 (cf. c. c. 151)

329. Madame Demolder as Toreador. – Aquarel, $10^1/_2 \times 13^3/_8''$. Collection M. Mabille, Brussels. p. 156

330. (c) Self-Portrait. – Pencil, $9 \times 6^5/_8''$. Ensor Museum, Ostend. c. c. 27

331. The Dispute. – Pencil, $9^1/_4 \times 11^3/_8''$. Collection G. Van Geluwe, Brussels. c. c. 151 (cf. p. 193)

1896

332. Flowers and Vegetables. – Oil on canvas, $31 \times 38^1/_2''$. Royal Museum of Fine Arts, Antwerp. p. 73 (detail), c. c. 113 (whole picture)

333. The Dangerous Cooks. – Oil on panel, $15 \times 18^7/_8''$. Collection R. Leten, Ghent. p. 290 (whole picture), p. 339 (detail)

334. Bric-à-Brac. – Oil on canvas, $15^3/_4 \times 12^5/_8''$. Formerly Buchholz Gallery, New York. c. c. 97

335. Combat. – Etching, $4^3/_4 \times 3^3/_8''$. p. 126 (cf. 1910 painting c. c. 162)

336. Triumph of Death. – Etching, $9^3/_8 \times 7^1/_4''$. p. 127

337. Small Persian Torture. – Colored pencil, $8^1/_4 \times 9^1/_2''$. Collection Claes-Boogaerts, Brussels, p. 155

338. (c) Cruel Joke on the Peasants. – Colored pencil, $7^1/_8 \times 9^1/_2''$. Collection A. Frey, Brussels. c. c. 160

1897

339. Masks and Death. – Oil on canvas, $30^7/_8 \times 39^1/_4''$. Museum of Fine Arts, Liège. p. 167 (cf. 1890 drawing c. c. 131)

340. Napoleon's Farewell. – Etching, $7^7/_{16} \times 4^{13}/_{16}''$. p. 124

341. Project for a Chapel Dedicated to Saints Peter and Paul. Pencil. Whereabout unknown. c. c. 198

1898

342. Ostend Rooftops. – Oil on canvas, $18^7/_8 \times 27^1/_2''$. Collection P. Pechère-Wauters, Brussels. p. 67

343. Seashells and Fish. – Oil on canvas, $32^3/_4 \times 40^1/_8''$. Private collection. c. c. 114

344. The Entry of Christ into Brussels. – Etching, $9^3/_4 \times 14''$. p. 125 (cf. 1888 painting pp. 181, 274/275)

345. The Vengeance of Hop Frog. – Etching, $14 \times 9^3/_4''$. p. 128 (cf. 1910 painting p. 225)

1899

346. Portrait of the Artist Surrounded by Masks. – Oil on canvas, $47 \times 31^1/_2''$. Collection Cl. Jussiant, Antwerp. p.165 (whole picture), p. 339 (detail)

247. Beach at Ostend. – Etching, $8^{13}/_{16} \times 11''$. p. 123

1900

348. Boats on the Beach. – Oil on canvas, $23^5/_8 \times 29^7/_8''$. Collection Mme. Van Weyenberg, Ressaix, Belgium. p. 273 (cf. 1892 painting p. 107 and 1888 etching p. 130)

349. Badgered Pierrot. – Oil on canvas. Whereabout unkown. p. 293

350. Skeletons in the Studio. – Oil on canvas, $44^7/_8 \times 31^1/_2''$. Collection E. Janson, Brussels. p. 295

351. (c) Azaleas. – Oil on canvas, $26^3/_8 \times 35''$. Royal Museum of Fine Arts, Antwerp. c. c. 124

352. (c) Plate in Embossed Leather. – Pencil, $8^1/_2 \times 6^1/_4''$. Collection P. Brusseleers, Antwerp. c. c. 237

1901

353. View of Mariakerke. – Oil on canvas, $19^5/_8 \times 25^3/_{16}''$. Royal Museums of Fine Arts, Brussels. c. c. 78

1902

354. The Antiquary. – Oil on canvas, $33^1/_2 \times 16^5/_8''$. Collection R. Desprechine, St. Denis-Westrem, Belgium. c. c. 10

355. The Canal. – Oil on canvas, $24 \times 29^1/_8''$. Collection Cl. Jussiant, Antwerp. c. c. 42 (cf. 1930 replica c. c. 43)

356. Gluttony. – Pastel, $4 \times 5^1/_2''$. Collection Colonel L. Franck, C. B. E., London. p. 158

357. Anger. – Pastel $4 \times 5^3/_4''$. Collection Colonel L. Franck, C. B. E., London. p. 158

358. Sloth. – Pastel, $4 \times 5^1/_2''$. Collection Colonel L. Franck, C. B. E., London. p. 158

359. Avarice. – Pastel, $4 \times 5^1/_2''$. Collection Colonel L. Franck, C. B. E., London. p. 159

360. Pride. – Pastel, $4 \times 5^1/_2''$. Collection Colonel L. Franck, C. B. E., London. p. 159

361. Lust. – Pastel, $3^3/_4 \times 5^1/_2''$. Collection Colonel L. Franck, C. B. E., London. p. 159

362. Study for Envy. – Pastel, $4^1/_2 \times 4''$. Collection Colonel L. Franck, C. B. E., London. c. c. 152

363. Study for Envy. – Pastel, $3^3/_4 \times 5^1/_2''$. Collection Colonel L. Franck, C. B. E., London. c. c. 153

1903

364. The Cook at the Billiard Table. – Colored pencil, $9^1/_4 \times 11^7/_{16}''$. Collection A. Taevernier, Ghent. p. 160

365. Louis XIV at the Billiard Table. – Colored pencil, $9^1/_4 \times 11^7/_{16}''$. Collection A. Taevernier, Ghent. p. 160

366. Napoleon at the Billiard Table. – Colored pencil, $9^1/_4 \times 11^7/_{16}''$. Collection A. Taevernier, Ghent. p. 160

367. Drunks at the Billiard Table. – Colored pencil, $9^1/_4 \times 11^7/_{16}''$ Collection A. Taevernier, Ghent. p. 160

368. Hitting the Cloth. – Colored pencil, $9^1/_4 \times 11^7/_{16}''$. Collection A. Taevernier, Ghent. p. 160

369. Skeletons Playing Billiards. – Tracing heightened with gouache, $11^7/_{16} \times 13''$. Collection Taevernier, Ghent. p. 161

370. Skeletons Playing Billiards. – Colored pencil, $9^1/_4 \times 11^7/_{16}''$. Collection M. Mabille, Brussels. p. 161

1904

371. The Virgin of Sorrows. – Oil on panel, $16^1/_8 \times 13^3/_4''$. Collection Claes-Boogaerts, Brussels. c. c. 199

1905

372. Double Portrait. – Oil on panel, $15^1/_2 \times 13''$. Collection Claes-Boogaerts, Brussels. p. 347

373. (c) Still Life. – Oil on canvas. Private collection. p. 283

374. (c) Temptation of St. Anthony. – Pastel, $4^7/_8 \times 7^1/_2''$. Collection G. Van Geluwe, Brussels. p. 155

375. (c) Frolicking Walkyrias. – Colored pencil, $7 \times 9^1/_2''$. Collection A. Frey, Brussels. p. 157

376. (c) Self-Portrait. – Pencil, $6^3/_4 \times 6^1/_8''$. Collection A. Frey, Brussels. c. c. 28

1906

377. Lady in Blue. – Oil on canvas, $29^1/_8 \times 23^3/_8''$. Private collection. c. c. 11

378. Ostend Rooftops. – Oil on canvas, $45^5/_8 \times 52^3/_4''$. Collection Dubois-Manne, Brussels. c. c. 84 (cf. 1884 painting p. 253)

1907

379. (c) Woman Eating Oysters. – Oil on canvas, $57 \times 43''$. Collection Cl. Jussiant, Antwerp. p. 257 (light version of 1882 painting p. 256; back dated 1882, done about 1907)

380. Chinoiseries. – Oil on canvas, $31^1/_2 \times 39^1/_4''$. Collection B. Goldschmidt, Brussels. p. 296 (cf. replica c. c. 98; there is another replica, dated 1908, oil on canvas, $14^1/_8 \times 16^1/_8''$, Collection Mme. M. Crick, Brussels)

381. Portrait of Mme. Emma Lambotte. – Oil on canvas, $18^7/_8 \times 14^5/_8''$. Private collection. c. c. 12

382. (c) Still Life with Chinoiseries. – Oil on canvas, $31 \times 38^1/_2''$. Royal Museum of Fine Arts, Antwerp. c. c. 98 (cf. p. 296)

383. Henri De Groux at the Billiard Table. – Colored pencil, $9^1/_4 \times 11^7/_{16}''$. Collection A. Taevenier, Ghent. p. 160

1908

384. Skeleton Musicians. – Oil on canvas. Private collection. c. c. 133 (replica, whereabouts of original unknown)

385. Ballet Dancers. – Oil on canvas, $33^7/_8 \times 28^3/_4''$. Collection R. Delhaye, Brussels. c. c. 170 (replica of 1895 painting c. c. 169)

1909

386. (c) Flowers. – Oil on canvas, $45^1/_4 \times 32^1/_2''$. Kröller-Müller Museum, Otterlo, Holland. c. c. 123

1910

387. (c) Afternoon at Ostend. – Oil on canvas, $51 \times 62^3/_4''$. Collection G. Daelemans, Brussels. p. 222 (light version of 1881 painting pp. 53 and 55)

388. (c) The Vengeance of Hop Frog. – Oil on canvas, $44^3/_4 \times 32''$. Kröller-Müller Museum, Otterlo, Holland. p. 225 (dated 1896, but it has probably been back-dated, and was actually done about 1910; cf. 1898 etching p. 128)

389. Still Life with Lantern. – Oil on canvas, $21^1/_2 \times 25^5/_8''$. Collection E. Bock, Brussels. c. c. 99

390. Still Life with Duck. – Oil on canvas, $31^1/_2 \times 39^3/_8$". Private collection. c. c. 115 (replica of a 1880 painting, oil on canvas, $31^1/_2 \times 39^1/_4$", in the Museum of Fine Arts, Tournay)

391. (c) Still Life with Fruits. – Oil on canvas, $8^3/_8 \times 13$". Collection Claes-Boogaerts, Brussels. c. c. 116

392. (c) Combat. – Oil on canvas, $23^3/_4 \times 19^3/_4$". Kröller-Müller Museum, Otterlo, Holland. c. c. 162 (cf. 1896 etching p. 126)

393. (c) Little Gathering in a Park. – Oil on panel, $5^1/_2 \times 7^1/_8$". Collection M. Mabille, Brussels. c. c. 184

394. (c) The Beach. – Colored pencil, $4^7/_8 \times 7^1/_2$". Print Room, Brussels. c. c. 54

1911

395. Intrigue. – Oil on canvas, $43^3/_4 \times 37^1/_4$". Collection A. Croquez, Paris. c. c. 134 (replica of 1890 painting p. 85)

396. Fifrelin (figure for The Game of Love). – Colored pencil, $12^5/_8 \times 9^5/_8$". Private collection. c. c. 176

397. Brutonne (figure for The Game of Love). – Colored pencil, $12^5/_8 \times 9^5/_8$". Private collection. c. c. 177

398. Miami (figure for The Game of Love). – Colored pencil, $12^5/_8 \times 9^5/_8$". Private collection. c. c. 178

1912

399. The Annunciation. – Colored pencil on paper. Private collection. c. c. 200

1913

400. Procession of the Penitents at Furnes. – Oil on canvas, $51^1/_8 \times 65^3/_4$". Marlborough Fine Art, Ltd., London. c. c. 201

401. The Raising of the Cross. – Conté crayon. Private Collection. p. 146

402. The Massacre of the Innocents. – Pencil. Private collection. c. c. 161

403. War of the Snails. – Colored pencil, $21^1/_4 \times 19^5/_8$". Collection B. Goldschmidt, Brussels. c. c. 163

1914

404. Figures in Front of a Poster for the Game of Love. (Elaboration of a motif from The Entry of Christ into Brussels). – Oil on canvas, $34^1/_4 \times 27^7/_8$". Collection B. Goldschmidt, Brussels. c. c. 135

405. Decor for the artist's ballet, The Game of Love (setting for the 2nd Act). – Oil on canvas, $66^1/_8 \times 81^1/_8$". Ensor Museum, Ostend. c. c. 179

406. Small Theater. – Oil on canvas, $14^5/_8 \times 18^1/_8$". Collection Claes-Boogaerts, Brussels. c. c. 172

407. (c) The Germans in Belgium (1914–18). – Colored pencil, $5^3/_4 \times 9$". Collection Claes-Boogaerts, Brussels. c. c. 147

408. (c) The Germans in Belgium (1914–18). – Colored pencil, $5^3/_4 \times 9$". Collection Claes-Boogaerts, Brussels. c. c. 148

409. Delights of Winter. – Colored pencil, $18^7/_3 \times 14^3/_8$". Formerly collection Mme. R. Daveluy, Ostend. c. c. 164

410. Decor for the artist's ballet, The Game of Love. – Colored pencil, $9^1/_2 \times 11^3/_4$". Collection A. Taevernier, Ghent, c. c. 180

1915

411. The Artist's Mother in Death. – Oil on panel, $9^3/_8 \times 7$". Collection M. Mabille, Brussels. p. 354

412. (c) Seascape. – Oil on a palette, $9^1/_2 \times 12^5/_8$". Collection P. Brusseleers, Antwerp. c. c. 62

413. (c) The Despair of Pierrot. – Oil on canvas, $26 \times 33^1/_{16}$". Kröller-Müller Museum, Otterlo, Holland. c. c. 132 (replica of 1892 painting p. 91; back-dated 1892, probably about 1915)

414. Unmasked. – Oil on canvas, $47^1/_4 \times 90^1/_2$". Collection Mme. Sacher-Stehlin, Basel. c. c. 181

415. Still Life with China Figurine and Pipe. – Colored pencil. Private collection. c. c. 101

1916

416. Bathers, Undulating Lines. – Oil on canvas. Private collection. c. c. 183

1920

417. Droll Smokers (Augusta Boogaerts und the painter Willem Paerels). – Oil on canvas, $29^1/_2 \times 25^1/_4$". Collection Claes-Boogaerts, Brussels. c. c. 13

418. (c) Carnival (after The Entry of Christ into Brussels). – Oil on canvas, $21^1/_4 \times 28^3/_4$". Stedelijk Museum, Amsterdam. c. c. 136

419. (c) Little Gathering in a Park. – Oil on panel, $6^1/_4 \times 8^5/_8$". Collection Claes-Boogaerts, Brussels. c. c. 185

420. Jesus Among the Doctors. – Oil on canvas, $20^7/_8 \times 29^1/_2$". Private collection. c. c. 202

421. (c) The Lamp Boy. – Oil on canvas. Whereabout unknown. c. c. 239 (replica of 1880 painting p. 33)

422. (c) Decadent Romans. – Conté crayon. Private collection. p. 153 (back-dated 1890, probably about 1920)

423. (c) La Sirène (Mlle. Boogaerts). – Colored pencil, $7^1/_2 \times 10^1/_2$". Collection Claes-Boogaerts, Brussels. p. 210

1921

424. Still Life with Cabbage. – Oil on canvas, $28^3/_8 \times 40$". Kröller-Müller Museum, Otterlo, Holland. c. c. 117

1922

425. Masks. – Lithograph, $14^7/_8 \times 21^1/_4$". c. c. 137

1923

426. (c) Self-Portrait. – Oil on canvas, $16^1/_2 \times 12^5/_8$". Uffizi Gallery, Florence. c. c. 21 (replica of 1879 painting p. 21)

1924

427. Moses and the Birds. – Oil on canvas, $49^1/_4 \times 49^1/_4$". Collection Baron A. de Broqueville, Brussels. c. c. 165

428. You Are Masks! – Colored pencil, $7^1/_4 \times 9^3/_8$". Collection P. Brusseleers, Antwerp. c. c. 139

1925

429. Andromeda. – Oil on canvas, $55^1/_8 \times 40^1/_2$". Collection Baron A. de Broqueville, Brussels. p. 285 (cf. c. c. 166)

430. Masks. – Oil on canvas, $21^5/_8 \times 27^1/_2$". Museum, Tel Aviv. p. 297

431. (c) Boat Aground, La Panne. – Oil on panel, $10^3/_8 \times 13^5/_8$". Collection G. Van Geluwe, Brussels. c. c. 35 (replica of 1876 painting c. c. 34)

432. (c) Delicacy. – Oil on panel, $8^5/_8 \times 11^3/_4$". Collection G. Van Geluwe, Brussels. c. c. 100

433. Red Cabbage. – Oil on canvas, $26 \times 31^1/_2$". Collection Claes-Boogaerts, Brussels. c. c. 118

434. (c) Banquet of the Starved. – Oil on canvas, $45^1/_8 \times 57^3/_8$". Collection Miss A. Milton de Groot, New York. c. c. 140

435. Infamous Vivisectors. – Oil on canvas, 24⅝×30¾″. Private collection. c. c. 154 (cf. drawing p. 156)
436. (c) The Deliverance of Andromeda. – Oil on canvas, 12⅝×9½″. Collection Claes-Boogaerts, Brussels. c. c. 166 (cf. painting p. 285)
437. (c) Bird Park. – Oil on canvas, 19¼×23″. Marlborough Fine Art, Ltd., London. c. c. 186
438. (c) Seashells and Mollusks. – Oil on canvas, 10¼×12⅝″. Private collection. c. c. 187
439. (c) Sick Tramp Warming Himself. – Oil on canvas, 27⅛×31½″. Whereabout unknown. c. c. 240 (replica of 1882 painting that was destroyed during World War II, p. 263)
440. (c) Infamous Vivisectors. – Colored pencil, 7×8⅝″. Private collection. p. 156 (cf. painting c. c. 154)
441. Christ. – Colored pencil. Private collection. c. c. 203
442. (c) Sick Tramp Warming Himself.–Charcoal. Private Collection. p. 183

1926

443. Physicians Belaboring a Fat Girl. – Colored pencil, 10⅝×14″. Collection Claes-Boogaerts, Brussels. c. c. 155

1927

444. Portrait of Mme. C. – Oil on panel, 27⅝×23⅝″. Collection A. Croquez, Paris. c. c. 14
445. (c) Masks. – Oil on panel, 7⅛×9¹³/₁₆″. Collection G. Van Geluwe, Brussels. c. c. 138
446. The Temptation of St. Anthony. – Oil on canvas, 23¾×27¾″. Private collection. c. c. 204

1928

447. Portrait of Monsieur X. – Oil on canvas, 27³/₁₆×20⅞″. Private collection. c. c. 15
448. Portrait of Carol Deutsch. – Oil on canvas, 25⅝×21¼″. Formerly collection C. Deutsch, Brussels. c. c. 16
449. (c) Flowers and Masks. – Oil on canvas, 21½×26″. Private collection. c. c. 125 (probably a falsification)

1929

450. (c) Page from a Notebook. – Pencil. Private collection. p. 342
451. Self-Portrait. – Pencil, 7⅛×4¾″. Royal Museums of Fine Arts, Brussels. c. c. 29

1930

452. (c) Lady Resting (Augusta Boogaerts). – Oil on canvas, 24×29½″. Collection Claes-Boogaerts, Brussels. c. c. 17
453. (c) Portrait of Mlle. Augusta Boogaerts. – Oil on panel, 8⅝×6¼″. Collection Claes-Boogaerts, Brussels. c. c. 18
454. (c) Ensor Surrounded by Masks. – Oil on canvas, 37¼×37¼″. Collection G. Niels, Brussels. c. c. 30
455. (c) The Canal. – Oil on canvas, 19¾×23⅝″. Museum, Tel Aviv. c. c. 43 (replica of 1902 painting c. c. 42)
456. (c) The Studio of the Artist. – Oil on canvas, 33×26″. Boymans Museum, Rotterdam (Collection D. G. van Beuningen). c. c. 89
457. (c) Dahlias. – Oil on canvas, 25¾×19⅞″. Collection G. Van Geluwe, Brussels. c. c. 126
458. (c) The Stranger. – Oil on canvas, 23⅝×31½″. Private collection. c. c. 141 (after The Entry of Christ into Brussels)

459. (c) Lady Godiva. – Oil on panel, 10⅜×6⅞″. Collection G. Van Geluwe, Brussels. c. c. 167 (cf. 1933 etching p. 126)
460. Queen of the Ballet with Wreath of Flowers. – Oil on canvas, 12⅝×15¾″. Collection Baron A. de Broqueville, Brussels. c. c. 173
461. Queen of the Ballet. – Oil on panel, 12⅝×15¾″. Collection Baron A. de Broqueville, Brussels. c. c. 174

1931

462. (c) Seashells. – Oil on canvas, 19⅝×23⅝″. Museum of Fine Arts, Liège. c. c. 119
463. (c) Mona Lisa Among Masks. – Oil on canvas, 24×18⅞″. Private collection. c. c. 142

1932

464. (c) Priapus Caressed. – Oil on canvas, 19⅝×13¾″. Collection G. Oschinsky, Brussels. c. c. 168

1933

465. Ensor at the Harmonium. – Oil on canvas, 31½×39¼″. Collection P. Croquez, New York. p. 217 (whole picture), p. 338 (detail)
466. Port of Ostend, Twilight in Stormy Weather. – Oil on canvas, 32¼×39¼″. Collection Mme. A. Croquez, Paris, p. 223
467. Lady Godiva. – Etching, 4⅞×3½″. p. 126 (cf. 1930 painting c. c. 167)

1935

468. (c) Dunes, Sea, and Ships. – Oil on canvas, 19¾×23⅝″. Collection G. Van Geluwe, Brussels. c. c. 47 (replica of 1876 painting c. c. 46)
469. Flowers, Fruits, and Sniffing Masks.–Oil on panel, 5½×7⅛″. Collection Baron A. de Broqueville, Brussels. c. c. 120
470. (c) The Dance of Daisies. – Oil on canvas, 21¼×25⅝″. Private collection. c. c. 175

1937

471. (c) Ensor with Palette. – Oil on panel, 12×11″. Collection P. de Weissenbruch, Brussels. p. 298 (whole picture), p. 338 (detail)

1938

472. Interior with Three Portraits. – Oil on canvas, 19⁹/₁₆×23⅝″. Collection Claes-Boogaerts, Brussels. c. c. 90 (cf. the photograph p. 351)
473. (c) Avenue de la Chasse, Brussels. – Colored pencil, 7⅞×5¾″. Collection Claes-Boogaerts, Brussels. c. c. 85
474. (c) Avenue de la Chasse, Brussels. – Colored pencil, 7⅞×5¾″. Collection Claes-Boogaerts, Brussels. c. c. 86

1939

475. Ensor the Musician in the Key of G. – Oil on panel, 7⅛×5½″. Collection Mme. L. Légrand, Brussels. c. c. 31
476. The Procession of St.Godelieve at Ghistelles.–Oil on canvas, 57⅛×45¼″. Collection A. Croquez, Paris. c. c.205

1940

477. (c) Self-Portrait. – Pencil, 4½×6⅞″. Collection Claes-Boogaerts, Brussels. p. 162

ACKNOWLEDGMENTS

We wish to thank the following persons for their valuable assistance in the preparation of this book: The organization Les Amis de James Ensor and, particulary, its president, Madame Léon Wielemans-Hennet, and the secretary Monsieur Jean Stevo.

Mesdames Jeannie Demany, Alex Daveluy, Emma Lambotte, and Albert Croquez; Baroness Lambert; Mesdames A. Marteaux, B. Serruys Van Sieleghem, and J. L. Wodon-Rousseau.

The Directors and Curators of the Ensor Museum, Ostend; the Musée National d'Art Moderne, Paris; the Kröller-Müller Museum, Otterlo; the Museum of Modern Art, New York; the Royal Museum of Fine Arts, Antwerp; the Royal Museums of Fine Arts, Brussels; the Museum of Fine Arts, Ghent; the Museum of Fine Arts, Liège; the Museum Municipal, Amsterdam.

Messieurs Jean Bauwens, Louis Bogaerts, Claes-Boogaerts; Baron De Brocqueville; Messieurs Herman Colson, Pierre Croquez, Georges Daelemans, Robert Desprechins, Louis Franck, André Gloeckner, Bénédict Goldschmidt, Fernand C. Graindorge; Baron Charles Janssen; Monsieur Cléomir Jussiant; Count Paul de Launoit; Messieurs Roland Leten, Marcel Mabille, Oscar Mairlot, Paul Pechère-Wauters, Gilbert Périer, Sam Salz, Jean Speth, Auguste Taevernier, Gustave Van Geluwe, Ernest Van Zulyen, Pierre de Weissenbruch. Special thanks are due to Monsieur Georges Willems (Gallery Georges Giroux, Brussels) for his personal help and for putting at our disposal a great part of the black-and-white illustrations.

Albert, king of Belgium 219, 367
Alpaerts, Flor 367
Apollinaire, Guillaume 191
Artan, Louis 92, 93, 105, 363
"Art contemporain" 358, 366
"Art, Moderne, L" 41, 92, 364

Balzac, Honoré de 42, 220
Barr, Alfred H. 26, 76, 92
Baudelaire, Pierre-Charles 42, 53, 230
Bazaine, Jean 79
Beardsley, Aubrey 109
Beckett, Samuel 184
Beers, Jan van 190
Berghe, Frits van den 232
"Blaue Reiter, Der" 12
Bonnard, Pierre 72, 95, 112, 231
Boogaerts, Augusta (La Sirène) 210,
    211, 212, 213, 220, 364, 365
Bosch, Jerome 76, 95, 109, 165, 173,
    190, 191, 200, 232
Botticelli, Sandro 179
Braekeleer, Henri de 95, 358
Braque, Georges 367
Bruegel, Pieter the Elder 11, 95, 109,
    173, 190, 191
Brusselmans, Jean 232
Burne-Jones, Edward 110, 202

Callot, Jacques 42, 76, 112, 191
Camp, Camille van 80
Cassou, Jean 26
Cervantes, Miguel de 42
Cézanne, Paul 24, 27, 58, 101, 194, 231
Chagall, Marc 227, 367
Chainaye, Achille 92, 93, 363
Champal 111
Charlet, Frantz 93, 362, 363
Chirico, Giorgio de 367
Christina of Sweden 226
"Chrysalide, La" 92, 93, 110, 363
Claus, Emiel 195
Cocteau, Jean 23
Colin, Paul 366
Constable, John 42
Corneille, Pierre 227
Corot, Jean-Baptiste 212
Courbet, Gustave 95
Crespin, Adolphe 41, 362
Croquez, Albert 367
Cros, Charles 99

Daeye, Hippolyte 232
Dali, Salvador 367
Daumier, Honoré 42, 191
Daveluy, Alexandra 365
Degas, Edouard 60, 194
Delacroix, Eugène 42, 194

Delattre, Louis 207
Delcroix, Léon 366
Delteil, Loys 366
Delvin, Jean 363
Demolder, Eugène 80, 189, 207, 363,
    364, 365, 366
Denis, Hector 129
Denis, Maurice 194
Descartes, René 226
Des Ombiaux, Maurice 207
Doré, Gustave 112
Dubar 362
Dubois, Paul 92, 93, 363
Dufy, Raoul 48, 69, 95
Dumesnil, Louise 81
Dürer, Albrecht 112
Duyck 362

Eekhoud, Georges 364
Einstein, Albert 359
Elizabeth, queen of Belgium 367
Elskamp, Max 180, 207
Ensor, Frédéric-James 24, 31, 38 f., 40,
    60, 65, 108, 211, 362, 364
Ensor, Maria-Catharina 31, 54, 60, 65,
    108, 211, 362, 366
Ensor, Mariette (Mitche) 38, 43, 54, 56,
    60, 65, 90, 211, 362, 365, 367
Ernst, Max 367
"Essor, L'" 92, 363
Evrard 41

Fantin-Latour, Théodore 68
Fétis, Edouard 189, 201
Fierens, Paul 27, 367
Finch, Willy A. 52, 60, 62, 93, 363
Flaubert, Gustave 76
France, Anatole 219
Franck, François, 357, 358, 366, 367
Frise 129

Gallait, Louis 191
Garvens-Garvensburg, Herbert von 366
Gauguin, Paul 12, 110, 179, 179, 195,
    231
Gavarni, pseudonym of Sulpice-Guil-
    laume Chevalier named 112
Gelée, Claude (Claude Lorrain) 129
Gezelle, Guido 209
Goethals, Ch. 363
Gogol, Nicolaj 197
Goya y Lucientes, Francisco José 14,
    22, 42, 61, 109, 112, 232
Grandville, Jean-Ignace-Isidore-Gérard
    191
Greco, El 179
Groux, Henri de 366
Grünewald, Mathias 227, 232

Haegheman, Léopold 366
Haegheman, Maria-Catherina see Ensor,
    Maria-Catherina
Haegheman, Marie-Louise (Mimi) 38, 65,
    211, 366
Hals, Frans 42, 197
Hannon, Théo 41, 60, 80
Hartung, Hans 79
Hecke, Paul-Gustave van 366
Heine, Heinrich 42
Hogarth, William 109
Hokusai 95
Huizinga, Johan 98
Huyghe, René 27, 84
Huysmans, Joris-Karl 99

Ingres, Jean-Auguste-Dominique 194

"Jeune Belgique, La" 41, 92
Joyce, James 188

Kafka, Franz 188
Kandinsky, Wassily 12
Khnopff, Fernand 41, 93, 202, 362, 363
Klee, Paul 367
Kôrin, Ogata 101
Kuyck, van 362

Laermans, Eugène 182, 195
Laforgue, Jules 53, 212
Lagye, Gustave 111
Lambeaux, Jef 363
Lambotte, Emma 365
La Tour, Georges de 22
Lautréamont, Isidore Ducasse, comte
    de 197, 212
Léger, Fernand 48, 227
Leman, Gérard-Mathieu 80, 111, 190,
    365
Lemonnier, Camille 64, 93, 207
Leonardo da Vinci 98, 191
Léopold II, king of Belgium 190
Le Roy, Grégoire 64, 205, 214, 366
Leyden, Lucas van 98
Lhote, André 194, 227
Liebermann, William S. 26
Lilar, Suzanne 99, 228
Lorrain, Claude see Gelée, Claude

Maeterlinck, Maurice 53, 207, 364
Magnasco, Allessandro 98
Maillol, Aristide 219
Malebranche, Nicolas de 226
Mallarmé, Stéphane 53, 212
Mandijn, Jan 232
Manet, Edouard 42, 48, 61, 68, 92, 95,
    112
Marquet, Albert 48

Matisse, Henri 68, 231, 367
Mauclair, Camille 64
Maus, Octave 92, 93, 190, 207, 363, 365
Meunier, Constantin 182
Michelangelo Buonarroti 129
Millet, Jean-François 42
Mimi see Haegheman, Marie-Louise
Mockel, Albert 207
Mollet, Ernestine 365
Monet, Claude 22, 48, 66, 101, 110, 195, 219, 231
Montherlant, Henri de 197
Monzie, Anatole de 367
Moreau, Gustave 41
Muls, Joseph 104
Munch, Edvard 12, 232
Murillo, Bartolomé Esteban 22

Nolde, Emil 366

Pantazis, Pericles 92, 93, 363
Permeke, Constant 34, 53, 105, 232
Picard, Edmond 93, 190, 364, 365
Picasso, Pablo 23, 109, 191, 231, 367
Pirandello, Luigi 166
Piranese, Giovanni Battista 112
Pissarro, Camille 109, 231
"Plume, La" 207, 364, 365
Poe, Edgar Allan 14, 188, 224, 230
Pollock, Jackson 79
Portaels, Jean 41, 362
Posada, José 112

Queneau, Raymond 197

Rabelais, François 42
Racine, Jean-Baptiste 209
Raphael 227
Ravel, Maurice 92
Reclus, Elisée 82
Reclus, Onésime 81
Redon, Odilon 26, 112, 231
Regoyos, Dario de 60, 363
Rembrandt, Harmensz van Rijn 14, 40, 42, 61, 69, 95, 99, 129
Renard, Jules 65, 214
Renoir, Auguste 27, 69, 109, 195, 212, 216, 231
Ridder, André de 26, 180, 366

Rimbaud, Arthur 65, 194, 197, 209, 212, 231
Robert, Alexandre 40, 362
Rodin, Auguste 93
Rops, Félicien 80, 92, 363
Rouault, Georges 231
Rousseau, Blanche 81, 207
Rousseau, Ernest (the elder) 80, 90, 129, 131, 190, 207, 210, 363
Rousseau, Ernest (the younger) 81, 82, 83, 90, 164, 189, 207, 210
Rousseau, Henri 98, 232
Rousseau, J.-B. 81
Rousseau, Mariette 80, 81, 82, 111, 166
Rowlandson, Thomas 108
Rubens, Peter Paul 11, 16, 165, 179, 232
Rysselberghe, Théo van 363

Sartre, Jean-Paul 188
Satie, Eric 197
Schlobach, Willy 363
Schneider, Pierre 65, 214
Schongauer, Martin 191
Schopenhauer, Arthur 227
Schwob, Marcel 94
Serruys, H. 367
Sérusier, Paul 178, 194
Seurat, Georges 92, 109, 110, 231
Severdonck, Jef Van 40, 362
Severini, Gino 191
Shakespeare, William 227
Shaw, George Bernard 219
Simons, F. 363
"Sirène, La" see Boogaerts, Augusta
Sisley, Alfred 231
Slingeneyer, Ernest 191
Smet, Gustave de 232
Spilliaert, Léon 105, 232
Stallaert, Joseph 40, 362
Sterling, Charles 58
Stevens, Alfred 43, 195
Stevens, Joseph 195
Stevo, Jean 367
Stobbaerts, Jan 358
Stravinsky, Igor 23
Strijdonck, Guillaume van 93, 363
Strindberg, Arthur 213
Sulzberger, Max 110, 189, 201

Taine, Hippolyte-Adolphe 212
Tan Hee Tseu 365
Teniers, David 76, 99, 109, 232
Teugels, Jean 37, 191
Thévenet, Léon 232
Titian 129
Toorop, Jan 92, 93
Toulouse-Lautrec, Henri de 72, 191, 231, 232
Turner, Joseph Mallord William 42, 66, 68, 95, 99, 101, 109
"Twenty, The" see „Vingt, Les"
Tytgat, Edgard 232

Utrillo, Maurice 216, 220

Valeriola, Edmond de 367
Valore, Lucie 220
Vanaise, Gustave 363
Van Dyck, Anthony 232
Van Gogh, Vincent 12, 27, 48, 53, 68, 72, 101, 109, 178, 179, 195, 212, 231, 232
Verhaeren, Emile 65, 180, 207, 208, 364, 366
Verhaert, Piet 363
Verheyden, Isidore 364
Verlaine, Paul 92, 207
Vermeer van Delft, Jan 98
Verstraete, Théodore 363
Vigny, Alfred de 197
Villiers de L'Isle-Adam, Auguste 92
„Vingt, Les" (Les XX) 24, 41, 62, 92, 93, 109, 110, 195, 207, 209, 363, 364, 365
Vogels, Guillaume 46, 60, 92, 93, 363
Vuillard, Edouard 13, 60, 231

Wagner, Richard 92
Wappers, Gustave 191
Watteau, Antoine 42, 95, 102
Wielemans-Hennet, Mme Léon 367
Wiertz, Antoine 80
Wilde, Oscar 230
Woestijne, Karel van de 207
Wouters, Rik 232, 366
Wytsman, Juliette 363

Yper, Auguste van 365